The media's watching Vault!
Here's a sampling of our coverage.

"For those hoping to climb the ladder of success, [Vault's] insights are priceless."
– *Money*

"The best place on the web to prepare for a job search."
– *Fortune*

"[Vault guides] make for excellent starting points for job hunters and should be purchased by academic libraries for their career sections [and] university career centers."
– *Library Journal*

"The granddaddy of worker sites."
– *The U.S. News and World Report*

"A killer app."
– *The New York Times*

One of Forbes' 33 "Favorite Sites"
– *Forbes*

"To get the unvarnished scoop, check out Vault."
– *Smart Money Magazine*

"Vault has a wealth of information about major employers and job-searching strategies as well as comments from workers about their experiences at specific companies."
– *The Washington Post*

"Vault has become the go-to source for career preparation."
– *Crain's New York Business*

"Vault [provides] the skinny on working conditions at all kinds of companies from current and former employees."
– *USA Today*

VAULT

THE MOST TRUSTED NAME IN CAREER INFORMATION

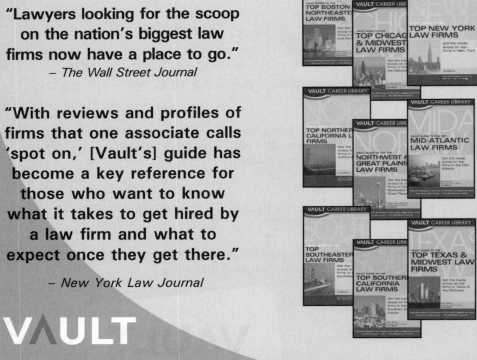

"Lawyers looking for the scoop on the nation's biggest law firms now have a place to go."
– *The Wall Street Journal*

"With reviews and profiles of firms that one associate calls 'spot on,' [Vault's] guide has become a key reference for those who want to know what it takes to get hired by a law firm and what to expect once they get there."
– *New York Law Journal*

VAULT

VAULT GUIDE TO THE TOP
INTERNET INDUSTRY EMPLOYERS

Use the Internet's
MOST TARGETED
job search tools.

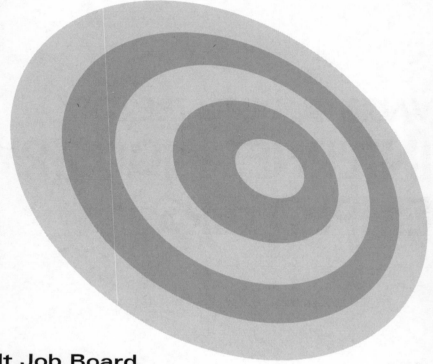

Vault Job Board

Target your search by industry, function and experience level,
and find the job openings that you want.

VaultMatch Resume Database

Vault takes match-making to the next level: post your resume
and customize your search by industry, function, experience
and more. We'll match job listings with your interests and
criteria and e-mail them directly to your inbox.

VAULT GUIDE TO THE TOP
INTERNET INDUSTRY EMPLOYERS

EDITED BY LAURIE PASIUK
AND THE STAFF OF VAULT

Library of Congress CIP Data is available.

ISBN 1-58131-384-5

Printed in the United States of America

ACKNOWLEDGMENTS

We are extremely grateful to Vault's entire staff for all their help in the editorial, production and marketing processes. Vault also would like to acknowledge the support of our investors, clients, employees, family and friends. Thank you!

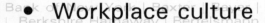

Table of Contents

INTRODUCTION

EMPLOYER PROFILES

Visit Vault at **www.vault.com** for insider company profiles, expert advice, career message boards, expert resume reviews, the Vault Job Board and more.

VAULT CAREER LIBRARY   ix

ABOUT THE EDITOR 256

Visit Vault at **www.vault.com** for insider company profiles, expert advice,
career message boards, expert resume reviews, the Vault Job Board and more.

V∧ULT CAREER LIBRARY   **xi**

Introduction

Introduction to the Internet Industry

Despite scars that remain from the "Bubble Burst" at the beginning of the century, the Internet continues to engage the imagination of businesses, consumers and information junkies across the globe. Today there are few aspects of modern life untouched by the Internet, an interconnected set of computers and networks fused together by copper wires and cables. More commonly, however inaccurately, when most people today refer to "the Internet," they mean the World Wide Web, an interrelated set of documents, files and data joined together by hyperlinks. One has to search far and wide to find an American business without a significant presence on the Internet, and the Web's seemingly unlimited real estate provides aspiring entrepreneurs the space to build their dreams upon.

Better to ask where it isn't

Its difficult to imagine many American lives untouched by the Internet. Today, home users can access the Web on dial-up telephone lines, landline broadband (via coaxial cable, fiber optic or copper wires), Wi-Fi, satellite and cellular phones. Public places, such as libraries, Internet cafes and airport terminals, offer immediate connection to those without home access and those who find themselves jonesing for the 'Net while away from their personal computer.

The ubiquity of the Internet in American life is unmistakable and on the rise. In 2005, nearly 70 percent of Americans, or 203.5 million people, were regular Internet users, an increase of 113.5 percent since 2000. The third quarter of 2005 found Americans spending more than $22 billion in e-commerce sales, just $6 billion less than was spent in online retail during the entire year in 2000.

E-commerce is centered in the capability to buy, sell and communicate online. Both web-specific retailers and established traditional brands have seen their share of success and failure as Americans become more accustomed to doing their shopping online. Despite the well-publicized failures of companies that made their way solely in e-commerce, for example, online grocery delivery services Webvan and Streamline.com, established

Visit Vault at **www.vault.com** for insider company profiles, expert advice, career message boards, expert resume reviews, the Vault Job Board and more.

V∧ULT CAREER LIBRARY

1

supermarket chains such as Safeway and Pathmark took note and began e-commerce online delivery shopping options.

Virtual success stories

Despite the failures of a vast majority of Internet start-ups, particularly in the pre-bust days in 2001, several companies managed to survive and become household names even when they lack any tangible product. These entirely virtual companies, such as eBay, Paypal and Google, mined gold from the essentially theoretical world of 1s and 0s that encompasses the digital realm. By making the complexities of information storage, retrieval, communication and trustworthy financial transactions simple for web-users, these companies have emerged as profitable examples of how the Web can be harnessed as a serious moneymaker.

A variety of options

When the Internet first became widely known in the mid-1990s, pundits predicted that its biggest successes would come from content, or web-based news and information sources. What took some time to figure out, and what is still under debate today, is how companies and web sites were to make money on information that was largely available for free. Throughout its brief existence, the Web has been most profitable in e-commerce and online advertising, though subscription-based content sites have shown some staying power of late, as have fee-based community forums and job boards.

Search and ye shall find

With a seemingly endless array of information posted on the Web, search engines provide a little relief. Google, launched in 1998, became the unmatched leader of search by 2001 and, in perhaps the ultimate brand accomplishment, has become a commonly used verb in the English language. In the last few years, several industry giants have looked to dip into Google's market dominance, as former Google client Yahoo! launched its own search engine in 2004 based on a number of acquired companies and technologies, and MSN Search, owned by Microsoft, which also relied on other companies to provide its search engine listings in the past. Search engines garner their revenue via ads targeted by keyword and sales of advertising placement to affiliated web sites.

The business of keeping in touch

A significant part of profit on the Web comes from community-based sites that link like-minded users with one another, help connect friends with friends and help in the quest for that special someone. Community sites like Friendster, an online social networking community that links trusted "friendsters" and the leisure entertainment they enjoy, and Myspace.com, another online community that allows its members to upload personal music, blogs and pictures, are free to their members and earn revenue through banner advertisements and product placement including faux-profiles of rock bands and movie characters. Fee-based services such as classmates.com and ancestry.com connect users to former classmates and information about family members, while dating services such as match.com and lavalife.com link the lovelorn with potential mates.

The retail that wags the dog

The Internet has long been touted as the future of retail, yet only within the last several years has that prophecy been fulfilled by companies actually posting profits instead of promise and potential. Revenue continues to rise for online companies of all stripes, including B2C (business to customer) sites such as renaissance vendor Amazon.com and DVD-rental titan Netflix, auction sites such as eBay and B2B (business to business) sites that use automated processes to link trading partners. Many e-commerce sites combine principles of other forms of Internet business, for instance, travel sites like Orbitz, Travelocity and Priceline, are operated like search engines that allow users to search for low-priced airfares, travel accommodation and car rental.

All the news that's fit to code

Despite the rise of blogs and myriad web sites that produce original content for free and make their earnings the "old fashioned way," i.e., banner advertisements and links to B2C sites, a growing number of sites have found success in a sector once thought to be financial suicide—online content for paying subscribers. Certain sites, such as the online magazine Salon.com are exclusive to the Web; others, such as espn.com's Insider content and *The New York Times*' new TimesSelect option, which provides subscribers with online access to the paper's columnists and archived articles for a fee. As more and more Americans switch from dial-up to broadband service, television and

Visit Vault at **www.vault.com** for insider company profiles, expert advice, career message boards, expert resume reviews, the Vault Job Board and more.

VAULT CAREER LIBRARY

3

movie studios are finding web-exclusive content increasingly profitable to a wider audience. In 2004, broadband penetration among Internet users grew to 55 percent.

Log on and drop out

Internet Service Providers (ISPs), the businesses and organizations that provide users with access to the World Wide Web and related services, necessarily change as quickly as the most recent technology. Witness the dramatic rise and fall of America Online, a titan of the dialup age that is struggling to keep pace as cable and wireless communications companies capitalize on the advances in broadband and Wi-Fi affordability and ease of use. While companies like PeoplePC, Earthlink and AOL survive with a focus on low-cost dial-up service, the days of dial-up connectivity appear to be numbered in the face of growing competition from subsidiaries of cable companies such as Comcast and Time Warner and cell phone outfits such as Verizon Wireless.

Content's time to shine

Now that major retailers have figured out how to reliably make money on the Internet, the next step in the Internet revolution is likely to be content-based. The technology appears in place to deliver television and movie content through the Web, potentially allowing content providers to eschew cable and satellite services to deliver programming directly to viewers. Companies like Microsoft and Cisco Systems' Linksys home division are hard at work on products that would facilitate Internet video to be viewed on TV sets instead of PC screens, and Apple's announcement in October 2005 that it would host episodes of popular network television shows for download to its iPod music player sent shockwaves through the entertainment industry. Internet search companies are beginning to test the video market, like the web-based video search service launched by Google in June 2005. Cable companies and phone providers such as Verizon and SBC that have entered the paid-TV market expect customers to increase demands for interactive content, and many are already offering on-demand programming which allows subscribers to download movies whenever they want. Still, most "traditional" content providers are reluctant to abandon television just yet. Comedy Central began an experiment in broadband-optimized content with the November 2005 launch of a unique site, MotherLoad, which offers select clips of content, but is intended to complement the cable station rather than replace it.

Online, or "new," media, is the nexus where all other media forms now intersect. Historically, technological innovation has defined the course of media advancement at the same time prompting fears in the already established of being rendered obsolete. While certain industries in "traditional" media, such as radio, television and print, saw the rise of the Internet as a harbinger of their demise, such has not been the case. Instead, just as with the rise of the printing press, radio, moving picture and television, conventional media forms have adapted to the new technology to maintain profitability and evolve to meet changing consumer tastes and expectations.

Several distribution methods have arisen in the past several years to fundamentally alter the creation of entertainment and media content on the Internet. Some, such as blogs, vlogs (video blogs) and podcasts, came from the underground, embraced by enterprising individuals, and picked up on by global corporations as a channel to new audiences. Others, such as mobisodes (content created for viewing on cell phones) and television episodes to be watched on iPods, take the entertainment technology breakthroughs of the past several years and inject it into a fully corporate, capital-intensive marketing and distribution plan.

Growth spurts

Online media forms are increasing in their ubiquity. More and more news hounds are getting their news online. A Nielsen/Netratings survey in June 2005 showed that one-fifth of regular newspaper readers have abandoned print newspapers, reading the news online almost exclusively. Another 7 percent split their reading between print and online reading. Initial statistics suggest a massive market for video downloads. In November 2005, Apple announced that customers at its iTunes Music Store had downloaded over one million videos since the company debuted the service in October, less than 20 days before. According to Technorati.com, a search engine popular amongst bloggers, the total number of blogs has increased from 8 million in March 2005 to over 24 million by the end of the year. At the beginning of 2006, some 20,000 podcasts were available on the World Wide Web.

Newsworthy times

The traditional news industry has been particularly affected by the rise of new media outlets, particularly the increasing impact of bloggers who operate without the demands of capital investment, commercial concerns or the traditional ethical restrictions of conventional journalism. Certain networks have taken to the Internet to preempt potential criticism. By the end of 2005, all of the major networks had adopted features on their web sites to provide transparency to their editorial and production decisions. NBC anchor Brian Williams writes daily entries to his msnbc.com blog, the *Daily Nightly*, in which he discusses pieces under consideration for the nightly newscast, answers viewer critiques and takes personal blame for flawed and incorrect stories. *Public Eye* Editor Vaughn Ververs at CBSNews.com functions independently from the news department, posting videos of editorial meetings and garnering answers from executives about charges of bias. (CBS in particular learned the hard way about the influence of the blogosphere, when conservative bloggers began vehement criticism of a CBS piece on George W. Bush's military service during the 2004 campaign that relied on documents that could not be authenticated.) Network execs explain that in the current information environment, a 22-minute nightly newscast is simply inadequate.

Watch that phone!

With the arrival of third-generation cellular services, the broadcasting and viewing of video footage on mobile television screens has become a realistic commercial possibility. 3G, short for third-generation mobile telephone technology, enables the transfer of both voice data (a phone call) and non-voice data (downloading information, sending e-mail, instant messaging, etc.). Large media corporations have been quick to offer material produced specifically for mobile phones, beginning with Twentieth Century Fox, which announced plans in November 2004 to create a unique series of 24 one-minute episodes (or "mobisodes") based on its popular show *24* offered exclusively on a new high-speed service by Vodaphone, the world's largest cell phone provider at the time. The new Vodaphone service would also provide trailers and clips of new movies, as well as news, sports, music and games. The launch came several years after Vodaphone spent billions for licenses to use a larger amount of public airwaves to deliver the high-volume content.

Playing video games

The rapid growth of vlogs (think a blog in video form) and web sites offering downloadable video podcasts seems to indicate that more and more people have lost interest in commercial television offerings, willing to seek out alternative broadcasting online or make their own programs. In December 2004, there were a mere two dozen active vlogs; by the time Apple added "Video Podcast" to the menu of the new video iPod, vlogmap.org linked to 415 vlogs worldwide; by early December 2005, mefeedia.com, a site allowing viewers to watch and subscribe to blogs worldwide, reported "2,017 vlogs and counting." Like their print cousin, most vlogs tend to be personal diaries and reflections that read as exercises in self-absorption, yet several sites have figured out that money can be made. For example, the daily three-minute fake TV news report *Rocketboom*, shot on digital video and edited on a laptop (costing around $20 an episode), attracts over 100,000 people per day, an audience roughly equivalent of many cable TV news programs. The two-person team behind *Rocketboom* signed a deal with TiVo in December 2005 allowing TV viewers to watch the web video on their home sets, and industry pundits believe that at its current viewership, *Rocketboom* could charge around $8,000 for an interactive ad at the end of the show, amounting to some $2 million annually.

Ad-aware

With at least 24 million blogs in America, every possible subject is likely to be covered, including rhapsodic tributes to favored brands. Take note, for example, of Michael Marx's online ode to Barq's Root Beer at thebarqsman.com, where he collects news about Barq's, analyzes its commercials and posts pictures of "Barq's Drinker of the Week." Though Barq's owner Coca-Cola may have been ignorant of Marx's site, other companies are exploring the blogosphere as a new advertising arena. Public relations firms are seeing these blogs as an immediate window into customer feedback and the opinions of a brand's largest fans provide an unprecedented glimpse into consumer preference. With more and more consumers expressing skepticism about product information provided to them by corporations, marketers see the unbiased opinion expressed on product-centric blogs filling a niche in high demand.

Word spreads fast

Beacons of traditional media have clearly taken notice of the success of new media. In December 2005, the National Academy of Television Arts & Sciences announced the creation of an award for Outstanding Achievement in Content for Non-Traditional Delivery Platforms to be presented at the 33rd Annual Daytime Emmy Awards in April. The organization originally planned to give out the award in May 2006 at the annual Sports Emmy Awards to acknowledge the best sports-related new media program, with entertainment not scheduled to be judged until 2007. Yet once made public in November 2005, the new category garnered almost a million hits on Google, and the academy opted to reopen the entry period in time for the 2006 Daytime Emmys.

The newest model

Programming created for traditional media has also found its way to new platforms. ABC's hit deserted-island drama *Lost* perhaps best illustrates the various applications of new media outlets. Fans of the show can watch it on TV, on DVR, on iPod ($1.99 an episode) and on DVD. For more, they hit the Internet and find hundreds of sites dedicated to the program, some created by ABC or the show's producers and some by rabid fans. Original content is created for web sites, blogs, DVDs, podcasts and books. Other networks are catching on. Writers of FX's *Nip/Tuck* have posted blogs on the web community myspace.com for the Carver, the show's resident serial killer, and writers for CBS's *How I Met Your Mother* contribute entries to a character's blog on the network's site.

Career tracks

Content creation: Content refers to the information and material displayed on a web page, created by writers and web producers and updated regularly to entice viewers into repeat site visits. Content includes articles, interactive applications, and downloadable and web-streamed music and video. The business model of some content-centered web sites, such as theonion.com and drudgereport.com, depend entirely on money generated by advertising revenue. Other sites, such as online magazine (webzine) salon.com, offer Internet surfers the opportunity to pay a subscription fee to avoid advertisements (either embedded or in "pop-up" form) while reading articles. The online content of established "old" media sites such as *Newsweek* or

CNN contain advertisements but also serve as an elaborate means of branding, bolstering awareness of their traditional product.

Marketing: Marketers work alongside both the sales force and content creators to develop original, cost-conscious and effective ways to promote a web site's content and services. Successful marketing campaigns begin and end with a single-minded focus on return to investment (ROI), looking to come out with more sales than money spent on marketing. As seen in examples above, marketing using new media has become increasingly complex, blurring the line between content and marketing, with faux blogs used to hype shows like *Lost*, actual consumer blogs dishing news about root beer and original episodes of television shows to further awareness of both network programs and new services available to cell phone users who upgrade their phones.

Product research: One of the truly unique benefits of online media comes form its capacity to provide immediate feedback from consumers. Online media outlets constantly monitor traffic to different parts of their web sites, reader comments and surveys, and discussion boards to understand what portions of their services are popular and which are unappealing. This immediate feedback greatly enhances marketing and sales strategic planning. Unlike gauging often imprecise television ratings or radio listener audience size, web content providers can immediately read the amount of times content has been downloaded, gaining instant insight into a product's popularity.

Design: Web design is arguably content in its own right, as its visual appeal defines the site using it. In fact, web page creation is recognized as an art form among some circles (most prominently by the Webby Awards, which have recognized web sites for their creativity, usability and functionality for 10 years now). There is high demand for designers trained in newer technologies such as Java programming and Macromedia's Flash programming languages, which facilitate the addition of streaming music and video to online media sites. While those looking to get involved as sales reps or content creators might not need to be directly involved in creating web pages, some familiarity with HTML or Photoshop can greatly enhance a resume and make advertisements and articles far more eye-catching.

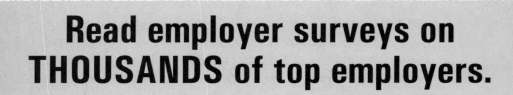

EMPLOYER PROFILES

About, Inc.

249 West 17th Street
New York, NY 10011
Phone: (212) 204-4000
Fax: (212) 204-1521
www.about.com

LOCATION

New York, NY (HQ)

THE STATS

Employer Type: Business Segment of The New York Times Company
President & CEO: Scott B. Meyer
2004 Employees: 90
2004 Revenue ($mil.): $35

KEY COMPETITORS

MSN
Wikimedia Foundation
Yahoo!

EMPLOYMENT CONTACT

jobs.about.com

THE SCOOP

One in five recommend ...

About, Inc.'s primary Internet portal, About.com, showcases a network of nearly 500 topic-specific web sites grouped into 24 content channels containing roughly 55,000 topics. Content is created by some 500 human "Guides," referred to as the "heart and soul of the About.com experience." The company generates revenue via advertisements on its site, which counts more than 20 million visitors on a monthly basis. Nielsen NetRatings consistently ranks About as one of the top 10 web properties in the U.S. In addition, the company is the single largest developer of original content on the Web.

Untangling the Web

About was founded by Scott Kurnit and a group of entrepreneurs in 1997 as The Mining Company with the purpose of compiling expert opinions on a variety of topics to help Internet browsers retrieve information quickly and effectively. TMC took on the moniker About.com in 1999 to reflect its growing cache of content and services. Publishing giant Primedia picked up About in 2001. Today, About operates as a business segment of The New York Times Company, which bought the firm from Primedia at the start of 2005.

The information authorities

About's band of gurus are typically experts in their fields, and, most often, have written books, appeared on national television and won awards. They are chosen for their ability to provide interesting information to users, as well as their passion for their subject. Competition is stiff — only 15 percent of those that apply actually make the cut for live service.

GETTING HIRED

About jobs

About typically offers jobs in content/guide operations, information technology, product management and sales. Available positions are listed on About's career site, jobs.about.com. Applicants are advised to e-mail a resume and cover letter, along

Visit Vault at **www.vault.com** for insider company profiles, expert advice, career message boards, expert resume reviews, the Vault Job Board and more.

VAULT CAREER LIBRARY   13

with salary requirements, to work@about-inc.com, with the preferred position in the subject line. For those who wish to become About Guides, application information is available at beaguide.about.com/applynow.htm.

ADVENTIS Corporation

10 Saint James Avenue, 17th Floor
Boston, MA 02116
Phone: (617) 421-9990
Fax: (617) 421-9994
www.adventis.com

LOCATIONS

Boston, MA (HQ)
New York, NY
Berlin
London
Shanghai

PRACTICE AREAS

Carrier Operations, Processes and
 Organization
Consumer, Small and Medium
 Business
Enterprise Solutions
Technology
Wireless

THE STATS

Employer Type: Private Company
President and CEO: Raul Katz

KEY COMPETITORS

Bartle Bogle Hegarty (BBH)
Huntsworth
Link ICA

EMPLOYMENT CONTACT

www.adventis.com/careers/careers.htm

Visit Vault at **www.vault.com** for insider company profiles, expert advice,
career message boards, expert resume reviews, the Vault Job Board and more.

VAULT CAREER LIBRARY

15

THE SCOOP

One chip, two chip, new chip, blue chip

Founded in 1993, ADVENTIS (formerly Renaissance Strategy) is a global consulting firm serving the new economy; in other words, the consultancy works with both "new chip" and blue chip companies in the telecom, technology and digital media sectors. ADVENTIS is quick to point out that it is not a generalist consulting firm; instead, the consultants call themselves "specialist advisors," bringing more than a dozen years of industry expertise to the table. The company breaks its business down into five main practice areas: carrier operations, processes and organization; consumer and small and medium business; enterprise solutions; technology; and wireless. The firm's services include strategy and positioning, growth and revenue generation, and operational and process excellence.

Small jewel

In March 2005, *Consulting Magazine* named ADVENTIS one of the industry's seven small jewels. In the years to come, the consultancy hopes it won't be so small. ADVENTIS Chairman and CEO Raul Katz told the magazine that he hopes to become an $80 million to $100 million enterprise. To accomplish this, Katz plans to continue to focus on the firm's core market, telecommunications in North America and the U.K., and to expand into new geographical markets, namely Europe and Asia. To better serve this new market, ADVENTIS opened outposts in Berlin and Shanghai in March and July 2005 respectively. The Berlin office is headed by Dr. Diethard Buhler, former management consultant for A.T. Kearney and Bain & Company. Jesse Parker, who has worked for IBM and Softbank International, and Cha Li, who served as president of Saatchi and Saatchi and brings more than eight years of investment and entrepreneurial experience in China to the firm, have been appointed to co-lead the Shanghai office.

The secret to their success

ADVENTIS grew its revenue 20 percent from 2003 to 2004. Katz says the secret to the company's success lies in three differentiating factors. First, the consultancy focuses on the board and C-level executives. ADVENTIS gains expertise from its board of advisors, made up of executives from organizations that have been clients at some point, which convenes a couple times per year. Second, Katz says that the consultancy has a great track record, which leads to a level of trust between the firm and its clients. And third, ADVENTIS prides itself on quality.

Insights

In addition to its consulting services, ADVENTIS is well known for its insight into trends and developments in the telecom, technology and digital media sectors. Its most recent observations—such as "Managing Technical Innovation" and "The New MNVO Game and How to Play It"—can be found on its web site. ADVENTIS consultants are also quoted in business publications such as the *Economist*, *BusinessWeek*, *The New York Times* and *Fortune*.

GETTING HIRED

Who, what, where and how

College graduates enter the firm as associates and MBAs typically join as consultants. ADVENTIS recruits from a select group of colleges, universities and MBA programs and seeks out individuals with an interest in telecom, IT and digital media. Interested candidates can also apply online via the career section of the firm's web site. ADVENTIS offers its employees the opportunity to work in small groups (typically three to six members), which means that even the junior associates have a wide range of responsibilities. Although employees work hard, a 50-60 hour workweek is the norm and consultants usually work on only one engagement at a time. Furthermore, although travel is part of the consulting biz, most travel for ADVENTIS is domestic. Advancement at this tech consultancy is based on merit and performance is measured semiannually.

Visit Vault at **www.vault.com** for insider company profiles, expert advice, career message boards, expert resume reviews, the Vault Job Board and more.

VAULT CAREER LIBRARY   17

Agency.com Ltd.

488 Madison Avenue, 22nd Floor
New York, NY 10022
Phone: (212) 358-2600
Fax: (212) 358-2604
www.agency.com

LOCATIONS

New York, NY (HQ)
Chicago, IL
Dallas, TX
San Francisco, CA
Amsterdam
London

THE STATS

Employer Type: Subsidiary of
Omnicom Group
Chairman: Chan Suh
CEO: Don Scales
2004 Employees: 398
2004 Revenue ($mil.): $103

KEY COMPETITORS

aQuantive
Digitas
Nurun

EMPLOYMENT CONTACT

www.agency.com/facts/careers.asp

THE SCOOP

It's all in the name

To understand the driving principle behind Agency.com, look no further than its name—simply, agency dot-com. As the nation's largest full-service interactive marketing firm, Agency.com balances web development with online advertising. The firm has become known for its interactive marketing techniques, which include outdoor displays, mobile phones and interactive television. Agency.com is a subsidiary of advertising giant Omnicom Group, and maintains four offices in the U.S. and two in Europe. Global clients include 3M, British Airways, eBay, Hewlett-Packard, T-Mobile and Visa.

Integrating the Internet

Kyle Shannon and Chan Suh (who remains the company's chairman today) founded Agency.com in 1995 in New York City to integrate interactive technologies with web development and marketing services. The company quickly earned a favorable reputation, gaining work with big names like Deutsche Bank, Nike, Sprint and Texaco. Advertising giant Omnicom picked up on Agency's buzz and acquired a significant minority investment in 1996, fueling growth. 1998 featured three big buys, including the remaining shares it did not own in Online Magic, a media agency headquartered in London; Boston-based Interactive Solutions, which doubled Agency.com in size; and Eagle River Interactive, whose client roster included Compaq, Ford, Motorola, Sharp and Sun Microsystems. By the end of the year, Agency.com had grown to become the largest agency dedicated to Internet-based advertising agency, with 575 employees spread across eight U.S. based offices.

In 1999, Agency.com continued to grow. The firm picked up itraffic, thus adding to its online marketing offering, and also purchased Comenhagen-based interactive TV company Visionik, as part of a plan to enter the European ITV content and marketing business. Agency.com's biggest venture of the year, though, was completing its initial public offering in an effort to generate revenue and reach more clients. The strategy worked: that December, company shares closed at 192 percent above their initial office price, giving Agency.com a market capitalization of $2.6 billion.

Weathering the storm

The firm topped Wall Street consensus forecasts in the first quarter of 2000, posting a profit for the first time, on the strength of relations with global clients such as British Airways and Colgate-Palmolive. *AdWeek* magazine hailed Agency.com as the "Best Full-Service Interactive Agency." Meanwhile, the company announced it would enter into the Latin American and Pacific Rim markets by taking minority positions in Agency.com Korea and Quaxxar of Miami, essentially creating two joint ventures. It seemed as though Agency.com had nowhere to go but up. But, after the dot-com bubble burst following the advent of Y2K, stock plummeted to a new low of $9.63, a mere margin of its IPO value of $26. Chan Suh was unaffected by the news, claiming the bust was "a natural and necessary process" and the dot-com industry would emerge "leaner and meaner."

Leaner and meaner, indeed

A joint venture between advertising giant Omnicom and Pegasus Partners II, L.P. took Agency.com and its staff of 1,600 private once again in 2001. The growth spurt came to a grinding halt that May, though, after a widening quarterly loss forced the firm to cut 350 jobs, thus reducing its workforce by 25 percent. Next to go were offices in Atlanta, Woodbridge, N.J., and Boston, closed in 2002 and 2003 as part of a restructuring process. Things at Agency.com settled down by 2004: the company became a wholly owned subsidiary of Omnicom, secured over 20 new clients, acquired Exile on Seventh LLC, a leading online ad firm, and won over 40 industry awards, including top web design firm in Forester's "Web Design Agency Shootout" and "Interactive Agency of the Year" by *B2B Magazine*.

As the company reached its 10th anniversary in February 2005, CEO Don Scales launched a plan to create the most admired full service interactive agency by fully integrating itraffic, its online advertising arm, under a redesigned Agency.com brand. Agency.com also launched a new web site, displaying the firm's full service offerings and showcasing some of its award-winning interactive work. Though a lot has changed in ten years, Suh remains faithful to a core philosophy—namely, that "digital interactions must provide value and fit seamlessly into the entire customer journey"—to catapult his company into new directions.

GETTING HIRED

Location, location

Jobs at Agency.com are arranged by location on the company's career web site, www.agency.com/facts/careers.asp. Each listing offers a job description, qualifications and contact information.

Visit Vault at **www.vault.com** for insider company profiles, expert advice,
career message boards, expert resume reviews, the Vault Job Board and more.

V∧ULT CAREER LIBRARY   21

Alloy

151 W. 26th Street, 11th Floor
New York, NY 10001
Phone: (212) 244-4307
Fax: (212) 329-8460
www.alloymarketing.com

LOCATIONS

New York, NY (HQ)
Boston, MA
Chicago, IL
Cranbury, NJ
Los Angeles, CA

THE STATS

Employer Type: Public Company
Stock Symbol: ALOY
Stock Exchange: NASDAQ
Chairman & CEO: Matthew C. (Matt) Diamond
2005 Employees: 4,600 (full- and part-time staff)
2005 Revenue ($mil.): $402.5

KEY COMPETITORS

PRIMEDIA
Time Warner

EMPLOYMENT CONTACT

www.agency.com/facts/careers.asp

THE SCOOP

An ally for Y

Alloy bills itself as a direct marketing and services company aimed at the fast-growing "Generation Y" group, which covers preteens, teens and twenty-somethings born roughly between 1980 and 1995. The Alloy brand is spread through a number of multimedia devices, namely direct mail catalogs, print media, web sites, on-campus marketing programs and promotional events. Revenue is generated from merchandising, sponsorship and advertising; nearly 40 percent of Alloy's sales come from merchandise sales via its catalogs and web sites, which include www.alloy.com, www.delias.com (for girls) and www.ccs.com (for boys). The company plans to spin off its merchandising group division to shareholders in late 2005.

From snowboards to message boards

Jim Johnson and Harvard Business School student Matt Diamond founded Alloy Online in the basement of a Boston apartment in January 1996. The company began by selling snowboarding gear through a print catalog, and later introduced a basic e-commerce web site. When demand grew, the duo quit their jobs in finance at General Electric and starting working on Alloy full time, expanding the catalog's offerings to include a full range of clothing and accessories for teenagers. While over 90 percent of the fledgling company's revenue was from orders placed in the print catalog, Alloy was simultaneously developing its web site into a virtual wonderland for Generation Y, with chat rooms, message boards, advice columns and entertainment industry gossip. The online community debuted in March 1998; within six months, www.alloyonline.com had boosted sales at the company's apparel arm by an astounding 400 percent. By May 1999, the date of Alloy's $46 million IPO, Diamond and Johnson's company had moved to a new headquarters in New York City and boasted over 50 employees—not to mention more than $10 million in revenue.

Like, a totally cool database!

Alloy's reach into the teenage psyche is virtually unmatched. Reaching over 25 million teenagers a month, the company has information on teens' likes and dislikes, habits and behavior. Wielding such tremendous influence, Alloy has managed to strike key marketing partnerships with a variety of Fortune 500 companies such as Procter & Gamble, Kraft, Johnson & Johnson and Viacom, as well as entertainment

Visit Vault at **www.vault.com** for insider company profiles, expert advice, career message boards, expert resume reviews, the Vault Job Board and more.

VAULT CAREER LIBRARY   23

companies like Paramount Pictures, UPN Network, Dreamworks Pictures and MGM, among others.

Alloy redesigned its site in November 1999, introducing new multimedia features like broadband entertainment (courtesy of Scour.net), voice chat, and MP3 and video downloads. At the time, most of the company's revenue came from its print catalog—an estimated 20 million copies of which were mailed in 1999. As the Internet became increasingly enmeshed with teen culture, Alloy developed its e-commerce arm and online marketing capability. Alloy will introduce its online social network in early 2006. The company also owns and operates leading college web site www.collegeclub.com and www.careersandcollege.com. Alloy also has key online marketing partnerships with Ellegirl, eCrush, Habbo Hotel and Promspot

At the head of the class

With a rapidly growing fan base firmly in place, Alloy moved next to tap teens' literary leanings, acquiring 17th Street Productions, a producer and developer of media properties for teens, and Girl Press LLC, a publisher of nonfiction aimed at teenage girls; and developing the Alloy Books imprint through a partnership with Penguin Putnam Books for Young Readers. The company was renamed Alloy Entertainment in 2004. Alloy Entertainment produced many of today's top selling teen projects, like *Sisterhood of the Traveling Pants*, *Gossip Girl* and the *A-List*. They currently have over 20 projects in development for film and television, and were the executive producers of the successful *Sisterhood* feature film. Alloy Entertainment produces about 70 projects annually in partnership with major publishing houses.

By March 2001, Alloy had blossomed into an $80 million multi-channel marketing powerhouse. CEO Diamond likened his company to other successful media brands like MTV for its ability to "reflect rather than dictate" trends. Analysts praised the firm's unique blend of "the three Cs"—content, community and commerce—and its knack for selling merchandise from a number of brands, thus avoiding being pigeonholed by private labels, and even referred to Alloy as the Martha Stewart of the teen world. To draw on the growing number of overseas customers, Alloy began shipping to the U.K. and Germany, and developed a Japanese-language web site.

Conquering the market

In July 2001, the firm picked up CASS Communications, a provider of integrated advertising and marketing services for college and high school markets, followed by the November purchase of 360 Youth, another marketing company aimed at teens and coeds. Marketing was at the forefront again in 2003, as Alloy picked up On-Campus Marketing (OCM) Direct, which provides marketing business and university-endorsed products for college students ranging from linens to care packages to diploma frames. Two months later, the company announced it was buying its next-closest catalog rival, dELiA*s, for $50 million. For the fiscal year 2004, the dELiA*s buy forced down gross profit as Alloy cleared out non-apparel inventory from the merchandise business, but overall is expected to boost profit in 2005 as more synergies are realized and new dELiA*s locations open up.

Today, the company is a leader in nontraditional media and marketing services reaching 85 percent the Millenial demographic (ages five to 29) with a host of large-scale proprietary networks offering advertisers access to the youth market across multiple key platforms. Assets include over 100,000 advertising panels in-school and on campus, web sites receiving over 3 million unique visitors each month, print vehicles reaching 50 million young consumers annually, one of the leading college newspaper placement services, extensive custom and cooperative sampling programs and a proprietary 25 million name database.

GETTING HIRED

Can you handle the truth?

Alloy's web site claims the company is "always looking for a few good women and men," and suggests job seekers e-mail queries to jobs@alloy.com regarding position availability.

Visit Vault at **www.vault.com** for insider company profiles, expert advice, career message boards, expert resume reviews, the Vault Job Board and more.

VAULT CAREER LIBRARY   25

Amazon.com

1200 12th Avenue South
Suite 1200
Seattle, WA 98144-2734
Phone: (206) 266-1000
Fax: (206) 266-1821
www.amazon.com

LOCATIONS

Seattle, WA (HQ)
Additional offices across North
America, Europe and Asia.

DEPARTMENTS

Business Development and Sales
Finance and Administration
Human Resources
Information Technology
Legal
Operations and Customer Service
Retail Product Management and
   Merchandising
Software Development

THE STATS

Employer Type: Public Company
Stock Exchange: NASDAQ
Stock Symbol: AMZN
Chairman, President and CEO:
Jeffrey P. Bezos
2004 Employees: 9,000
2004 Revenues ($mil.): $6,921.1

KEY COMPETITORS

Barnes & Noble
Columbia House
eBay

EMPLOYMENT CONTACT

www.amazon.com/careers

THE SCOOP

Books and beyond

Initially advertised as the Earth's biggest bookstore, Amazon.com now offers the Earth's biggest selection. The Seattle-based company sells everything and anything, including CDs, movies, toys, software, household and home improvement items, clothing, video games, prescription drugs and gourmet food.

Founded in 1994, Amazon is the brainchild of Jeff Bezos, the company's chairman, president and chief executive officer. Back then, Bezos sought to solve a seemingly intractable problem: How can you stock a store with every book in print? When Bezos launched Amazon out of his suburban Seattle garage, the store had a catalog of 1.1 million book titles. In comparison, even the largest and most extensive of the "brick and mortar" superstores could only offer 175,000. Furthermore, Amazon's online catalog allowed visitors to easily search for books by author, title, subject or keyword. Within a month of its opening, book lovers from every state and 66 countries had made purchases from the site.

In 1998, Amazon started expanding its virtual aisles and never looked back. The online phenom's foray into online CD and DVD sales was an overnight success—in its first quarter in the music biz, the company raked in $14 million in revenue. In the same year, Amazon acquired U.K.-based Bookpages and German Telebooks, both Internet bookselling competitors, as well as Internet Movie Database, an extensive movie information site. With an eye on expanding its product offerings even further, Amazon purchased a minority stake in drugstore.com and introduced an auction site in an effort to compete with another e-commerce giant, eBay. Soon, Amazon moved even further away from its bookselling roots with its plunge into toys and consumer electronics.

A few failures along the way

Along the road to becoming the store that offers everything, Amazon met with a few failures. Living.com (an older company not to be confused with the new living.com site currently owned and operated by Scripps Networks, Inc.), in which the company had invested heavily, went under in August 2000. Furthermore, a joint partnership between Sotheby's and Amazon, creating a co-branded site, closed in October 2000. And in 2001, Kozmo, the delivery service to which Amazon had given a $60 million

Visit Vault at **www.vault.com** for insider company profiles, expert advice, career message boards, expert resume reviews, the Vault Job Board and more.

VAULT CAREER LIBRARY   27

shot in the arm, also flat-lined. As a result of these missteps, the firm was forced to cut its employment numbers by 15 percent in 2001.

Undeterred by these setbacks, Amazon's pattern of entering into strategic partnerships continued. In 2002, for example, the company reached agreements with two former competitors, CDNow and Virgin Megastores, to provide co-branded online storefronts. In that same year, Amazon also engineered partnerships with several clothing retailers, including the Gap, Nordstrom's and Lands' End. Under the terms of these alliances, the clothing companies own and deliver the merchandise, while Amazon operates the web sites and takes orders. In September 2003, Amazon gained a foothold in yet another market with the launch of its new sporting goods store offering thousands of items through alliances with sports retailers such as Sportsrus.com, Eastbay, eSportsonline.com and Baseball Warehouse—to name a few. More recently, in May 2005, the online behemoth introduced Amazon Wedding, a one-stop site destination for gift registry and wedding planning.

The path to profitability

While its revenue and products continue to grow, Amazon has finally overcome its struggles with profitability, earning net income for 2003 and 2004. The fourth quarter of 2001 was the company's first period of profitability (and its first billion-dollar quarter). The shift to black was due in part to some savvy promotional tactics as the company offered a 30 percent discount on books priced at $20 and above. The holiday season also swelled coffers and Amazon found that its global reach paid off smartly as international sales surged.

The elusive first profitable quarter did not, however, mean that Amazon was out of the woods. Indeed, the company fell back into the red in 2002—albeit with narrower losses than the year before. Then, in the fourth quarter of 2002, Amazon once again posted a profit and its overall loss for the year was reduced to just $150 million, down from $567 million in 2001.

Amazon's financial performance continued to improve in 2003. Bolstered by a weak dollar and the Harry Potter book-buying bonanza, Amazon beat analysts' expectations for the second quarter of 2003—though it still finished with a loss. The company sold 1.4 million copies of the fifth Potter adventure, *Harry Potter and the Order of the Phoenix*, and picked up 250,000 new customers in the process. In addition, the unusually weak dollar meant that foreign exchange rates added $55 million to net sales compared with the second quarter of 2002.

For the year, Amazon reported total revenue of almost $5.3 billion, a $600 million increase from the $4.7 billion it forecast at the beginning of the year, and net income of $35.3 million, marking the first time in company history when Amazon ended a fiscal year in the black. 2004 was another profitable year for the online goliath, which posted sales of $6.9 billion and net income of $555 million.

Beating the Street

Most recently, the company wowed investors by beating Street estimates for the first time in four quarters. For the second quarter of 2005, the company boosted sales 26 percent to $1.75 billion and posted net income of $52 million. Net profits actually decreased from the same quarter in 2004, but this year's figure included $56 million in income taxes, compared with $5 million a year ago. The company attributed the revenue increase to lower prices and free shipping. A large chunk of the earnings upside came from what Amazon calls "other revenues" in North America. This vague delineation includes sales from merchants who own and deliver their own merchandise, but use Amazon as an online home. Products from such merchants carry higher profit margins because Amazon doesn't have to stock them.

Spending spree

Still, industry experts are a bit wary about Amazon's spending spree. The company increased its expenditures on technology and content by nearly 50 percent from a year ago; marketing expenses shot up 24 percent. What's more, Amazon lost $45 million on shipping as a result of free-shipping offers on orders over $25 and a new customer loyalty program called Amazon Prime which grants customers free two-day shipping for an annual charge of $79. On the other hand, Amazon says it considers free shipping to be a marketing expense since its primary purpose is to attract and retain customers. In the long run, Amazon's CFO Tom Szkutak believes the strategy—spending money on customer incentives—will have future pay-offs.

GETTING HIRED

It's all online

Individuals interested in working for Amazon would do well to check out www.amazon.com/careers. The site is chock-a-block of employment information, including departments, work environment, company history, company values,

Visit Vault at **www.vault.com** for insider company profiles, expert advice, career message boards, expert resume reviews, the Vault Job Board and more.

VAULT CAREER LIBRARY   29

benefits, locations, university recruiting and interview tips. Prospective hires are encouraged to create an employment profile and apply online.

Two-step

According to Amazon, the interview process typically involves "one to two phone interviews with potential peers or the hiring manager" followed by an "on-site interview with five to seven people." Our sources report a similar experience. An associate remembers having "a brief phone interview" and "an in-house interview." A manager says he went through "numerous rounds of interviews with about three to four people interviewing each round," while an editor "met with four different people in my department, from the top editors to the vice president of the department, spending about an hour with each."

Do your homework

Amazon advises candidates to do their homework and research the company before their interview. Furthermore, the company says it's a good idea to request a copy of the job description, prepare some questions for the interviews, and have a pencil and paper available during the initial phone screening.

For the most part, insiders describe the interview process as "standard" and "run-of-the-mill," with questions like "What is your greatest strength?" An editor explains, "Mostly it seemed that they wanted to gauge my familiarity with the industry and what innovations I might be able to bring to the department." A programmer adds, "Amazon is looking for people with enthusiasm. Show your interest in your interview and do some research on the company ahead of time."

On the other hand, one source warns that, "It is by no means a fluffy interview where you can BS your way in." Another contact adds, "Be aware that the interviews are not easy and be prepared for tough questioning. Have facts, figures and clear explanations ready."

OUR SURVEY SAYS

Fasten your seatbelt

Insiders describe the corporate culture at Amazon as "very informal, but intense and fast-paced." Sources say the environment is not for everyone, but "it's a fun place to be if you can handle constant change and you like to think." Nay-sayers grumble about the detail-oriented culture and long hours, but their more upbeat colleagues point out that while the culture may be demanding, it is also "energetic, supportive, positive and casual." Adds one contact, "People assume that you are smart until you prove otherwise. There is little posturing in meetings where people try to make themselves look smarter or better than others. It is a professional work environment where people don't swear in meetings and pound on tables."

Hours: Better than before

Insiders report that the hours at Amazon are long. One source reports working, "55-60 hours per week" or "11-12 hours a day for five days per week." In addition, this contact puts in a "few weekends outside of the holiday season." Another former employee notes that "the hours were long and the expectation was that you had to work 60 hours a week minimum under salary." Still, sources observe that "it is not as intense as it was in 1999, 2000 and 2001." Individuals have more flexibility in terms of managing their own hours. One contact adds, "There's a lot of work to do and every time I turn around there's more going, but that just means priorities need to be juggled."

The sky is the limit?

One source reports that "if you're not afraid of work, the sky is the limit with Amazon." However, another contact says that "promises for internal advancement/development" never materialize, leading to high turnover. Yet another insider says that while "opportunities for advancement are available," Amazon tends "to go to outside hires with more experience and education."

America Online

22000 AOL Way
Dulles, VA 20166
Phone: (703) 265-1000
Fax: (703) 265-1101
www.aol.com

LOCATIONS

Dulles, VA (HQ)
Columbus, OH
Mountain View, CA
New York, NY
Additional locations worldwide.

DEPARTMENTS

Access Business
AOL Europe
Audience Business
Digital Services Business

THE STATS

Employer Type: Business Segment of Time Warner
Chairman and CEO: Jonathan Miller
2004 Employees: 15,500
2004 Revenue ($mil.): $8,692

KEY COMPETITORS

EarthLink
Microsoft
Yahoo!

EMPLOYMENT CONTACT

www.aol.com/careers

THE SCOOP

A quantum leap

With 21 million subscribers and $8.7 billion in revenue, AOL is the world's largest Internet access provider. Originally known as Quantum Computer Services, AOL got into the Internet access biz with a service called Q-link for users of Commodore computers. Under the leadership of Steve Case, the start-up added services for owners of Apple computers and IBM PC clones, quickly building up a presence in local markets. Industry experts lauded the small fry's success, but predicted the company would never be as big as rivals Prodigy and CompuServe. But by 1996, AOL had boosted its subscriber base to 5 million (and growing), surpassed CompuServe, and set its eye on becoming the No. 1 global consumer online service.

Today, AOL is about more than just internet access, providing its customers with a plethora of services, including information on sports, stocks, news and weather, chat groups, online forums with big-name experts and celebrities and online shopping. Recently, AOL added streaming audio and video content—including exclusive live concerts, celebrity interviews and film shorts—to the mix.

AOL abroad

While continuing to expand business at home, AOL turned its attention overseas. The company opened its virtual doors in Western Europe in 1996 and in Latin America in 1999. AOL Europe encountered problems early on, facing tough European competition and dealing with expensive European Internet connections. The unit finally broke even in September 2003. AOL Latin America, on the other hand, met with initial success, garnering 1 million subscribers and the title of "fasted growing Internet service provider in the region" by 2001. However, over the next few years, AOL Latin America failed to establish a strong regional base, with market share dropping from 10 percent in 2002 to 4.5 percent by early 2004.

Kid-friendly AOL

In September 2003, AOL launched "KOL," a kid-friendly version of the online service designed for six to 12 year olds. KOL Jr., for preschoolers, is also in the works. KOL, available to registered AOL members, features a welcome screen, tool bar and Buddy List that children can customize to their personal tastes, enhanced navigation capabilities, educational resources and original programming, as well as new safety features for parents. KOL includes content from kid-friendly venues, such as the Cartoon Network and DC Comics, and offers monitored chat rooms. The concept for KOL was born out of data suggesting 46 percent of kids under 12 access the Internet at least four times a week, and nearly 20 percent log on every day.

Hard times

In the years since its merger with Time Warner—the deal was completed in January 2001—AOL has seen its fair share of hard times. For one, the number of subscribers plummeted as customers took advantage of new broadband services offered by phone companies. In 2003 alone, the company lost 5 million worldwide subscribers, despite attempts to hedge losses with a new broadband—or high-speed—service of its own. The online business unit also faced a pair of investigations by the Securities and Exchange Commission for overstating advertising revenue and the number of subscribers between 2000 and 2002. By 2003, AOL was widely portrayed in the media as an albatross around Time Warner's neck, and in September 2003 the company made the executive decision to drop "AOL" from its name. The media conglomerate also switched its stock ticker from AOL to TWX.

In a related move, Steve Case stepped down as chairman of the company he had helped build. Case had come under fire from shareholders, board members and executives over the company's decline in stock price and federal accounting investigations, which dragged Time Warner down as a whole. "I love this company, and I would love to remain as chairman," Case said. "[This] is about what is best for the company." Case's resignation went into effect in May 2003.

For keeps

With all the negative buzz surrounding AOL, there have been rumors that Time Warner CEO Richard Parsons might sell the online albatross off. But insiders say Parsons told AOL employees the company is "for keeps." Earlier this year, Parsons forked over $500 million to settle SEC investigations into AOL and has announced that he is siphoning off an additional $3 billion to settle private shareholder suits related to the business unit. Experts have speculated that the chief executive wants to make sure AOL has a clean slate going forward. Furthermore, Parsons indicated he is willing to loosen the purse strings even more to allow AOL to make acquisitions to improve its online presence and attract revenue. And in July 2005, the chief executive told *BusinessWeek* he would consider a spin-off to give AOL its own equity to acquire new properties.

You've got content

In July 2005, AOL opened its virtual doors to the public. The move—providing content for free—is a gamble for the company, which has historically garnered most of its revenue—about 80 percent—from subscriber fees. But as the company continued to lose subscribers, it realized it needed to do something drastic. With content open to all, AOL throws itself at the mercy of online-ad dollars. With online-ad spending expected to grow from $10.7 billion in 2005 to $16.1 billion in 2009 according to Jupiter Research, industry experts say, there's plenty to go around. What's more, ads produce margins of 50 percent versus the 20 percent margins of subscription sales. Still, skeptics say that the move may be too little too late. AOL CEO Jon Miller told *BusinessWeek* in June 2005, "If we could have done it earlier, I would have been happier."

GETTING HIRED

Persistence pays

To find out about current job opportunities consult the "Careers" section of AOL's corporate site, located at www.corp.aol.com. In addition to sending a resume to human resources (which insiders say can be very slow), applicants are advised to network with people on the inside, as employee referrals are one of the largest sources of hires. The company hires people of all professional backgrounds; opportunities run the gamut from programming and software development to editing and writing. Whether you're interested in marketing or accounting, there may be a place for you at America Online—but technophobes need not apply.

AOL employees report that the company offers many entry-level opportunities, but that more advanced positions require "dogged persistence." They advise new employees to "be aggressive" and "make sure you have the projects that you want." Positions are available in the company's call centers, but in the corporate offices the best way for college students to get a foot in the door is through its summer intern program. For business school grads, the "easy access to VPs and sometimes even the CEO" can be very rewarding, although there is no set path of entry for MBAs.

The interview process typically involves an initial phone screening followed by a series of in-person interviews. Although candidates can expect a few technical or case questions, the majority of questions are routine. Says one source, "Behavioral questions are the norm." Another contact adds that the "questions were pretty standard, asking about challenges, strengths, weaknesses, etc."

OUR SURVEY SAYS

Computer geeks vs. money mongers

A quickly growing company, work at AOL can provide excitement, but it is also often disorganized and "chaotic." There is, however, a wide gulf between those working in finance or management and those in entry-level technical positions. While one MBA refers to his job as "remarkable," one of AOL's online technicians refers to the atmosphere as "sometimes cold-hearted."

Sleep is highly overrated anyway

Where hours are concerned, many employees report that they have flexible hours: "I'm not a morning person, so I usually do noon to 9 p.m. or so." "Personally, I set my own hours," says another employee. Flexible, however, doesn't mean short: "It's not uncommon for people to put in 60 hours a week," says one insider. Reports another: "The hours can be long, and can take a toll on your personal life, especially if you are on a track for increased responsibility." And: "The company only requires 8-hour workdays officially, but realistically, many people work longer hours than that." Employees attribute the long workdays largely to a culture of constant innovation: "It can be difficult for those who don't like to work hard, since we're always pushing ourselves to do things that have never been done before."

Who needs pay when you have ... uh ... satisfaction?

AOL employees are not as effusive when it comes to pay. "It certainly pays the bills and leaves me some left over to play," says one employee. "It's probably not the highest you'll find, but competitive," reports another insider. However, insiders say that AOL has a 401(k) plan that matches fifty cents on the dollar up to 6 percent of an employee's salary. Other perks include an employee stock purchase plan, a company gym, a "decent health plan" and a "free AOL account for you and one other person of your choosing."

Most important, however, is that most company insiders reported an extraordinary level of job satisfaction. "I still wake up in the morning looking forward to coming into the office," says one employee who has been with the company for four years. "Out of almost six years," says another, "there's probably been less than 10 days that I haven't looked forward to coming into work." Getting repetitive? "Overall, I've never regretted it," says yet another. "I can't imagine working anywhere else."

Visit Vault at **www.vault.com** for insider company profiles, expert advice, career message boards, expert resume reviews, the Vault Job Board and more.

VAULT CAREER LIBRARY

37

Ask Jeeves, Inc.

555 12th Street, Suite 500
Oakland, CA 94607
Phone: (510) 985-7400
Fax: (510) 985-7412
www.askjeevesinc.com

LOCATIONS

Oakland, CA (HQ)
Campbell, CA • Irvington, NY •
Piscataway, NJ • Los Angeles, CA •
New York, NY • Chicago, IL •
Dublin • London • Madrid • Rome •
Tokyo

DEPARTMENTS

Ask Jeeves
Ask Jeeves Kids
Ask Jeeves UK
Ask Espana
Bloglines
Excite
IWon
MaxOnline
MySearch
MyWay
MyWebSearch
Teoma

THE STATS

Employer Type: Subsidiary of
IAC/InterActiveCorp
CEO: Steven Berkowitz
2004 Employees: 505
2004 Revenue ($mil.): $261.3

KEY COMPETITORS

Google
MSN
Yahoo!

EMPLOYMENT CONTACT

www.askjeevescareers.com/askjeeve
s/jobboard/default.asp

THE SCOOP

The butler knows best

Ask Jeeves began as a search engine that "understood" natural language queries, and the answers to the questions were served via a proper English butler. Berkeley venture capitalist Garrett Gruener and software developer David Warthen are the brains behind the business, which was launched in 1996. The six-person startup underwent rapid growth in the first couple years of business, increasing its staff to over 300 by the end of 1999 and nabbing corporate clients like Microsoft, Dell and Toshiba. Today, having survived economic downtimes, Ask Jeeves is the seventh largest search company, with more than 40 million visitors per month, roughly 500 employees and $261.3 million in 2004 revenue.

The many faces of Jeeves

From butlers to bloggers, Ask Jeeves encompasses more than just its flagship site, www.ask.com. Related, but separate, are Ask Jeeves Kids, a site focused on "edutainment," which allows kids to search with keywords or questions such as "Why is the Sky Blue" and "Living in Space"; Ask Jeeves UK, launched in February 2000; Ask Jeeves Japan in 2004; and Ask Espana, launched in 2005. Ask Jeeves also operates a number of other sites, including IWon, Excite, MyWay, MyWebSearch and MaxOnline. Most recently, in February 2005, Ask Jeeves nabbed Bloglines, one of the world's most popular blog sites and one of *Time* magazine's 50 Coolest Websites for 2004.

A deal with Diller

In March 2005, Ask Jeeves announced that it would be acquired by IAC/InterActiveCorp, the media company headed by mogul Barry Diller. The price tag was $1.85 billion, considered by some to be a bargain at 16.5 times earnings, especially when compared to similar deals such as the New York Time Company's acquisition of About.com (23 times earnings) and Dow Jones' purchase of CBS MarketWatch (19 times earnings). Still, insiders say the move is a good one as Ask Jeeves complements IAC's other sites, such as Ticketmaster.com and Match.com. For Ask Jeeves, the deal with Barry Diller gives the small fry an opportunity to focus less on profitability and more on R&D and marketing investments. Charlene Yi, principal analyst at Forrester Research, says that industry watchers have been impressed by Ask Jeeves' ability to compete with the likes of Google and Yahoo!

Visit Vault at **www.vault.com** for insider company profiles, expert advice, career message boards, expert resume reviews, the Vault Job Board and more.

V∧ULT CAREER LIBRARY   39

considering the company's limited resources. Now, all eyes are on Ask Jeeves to see what its management and engineers can do with the resources IAC has to offer.

GETTING HIRED

Jeeves-of-all-trades

Candidates can search for jobs and apply online through Ask Jeeves' corporate web site (www.askjeevesinc.com). The company offers jobs in engineering, product development, accounting and finance, administrative, editorial, information technology, facilities, human resources, legal, marketing, professional services, sales, and training and documentation.

Bluefly, Inc.

42 West 39th Street, 9th Floor
New York, NY 10018
Phone: (212) 944-8000
Fax: (212) 354-3400
www.bluefly.com

LOCATION

New York, NY (HQ)

Visit Vault at **www.vault.com** for insider company profiles, expert advice,
career message boards, expert resume reviews, the Vault Job Board and more.

VAULT CAREER LIBRARY   41

THE SCOOP

Outlet shopping online

An online retailer of off-price designer clothes, accessories and housewares, Bluefly provides a fix for those with Prada tastes but Kmart budgets. Its web site offers a dizzying amount of merchandise (some 80,000 items) from more than 350 designer labels, including Gucci, Calvin Klein, Diesel and Donna Karan, at prices up to 75 percent off retail. The e-retailer differs in one respect from its brick-and-mortar outlet cousins: it only offers first-quality merchandise, which it buys both directly from the designers and from resellers at wholesale. (Outlets usually sell factory seconds and irregulars in addition to top-quality goods).

Bluefly founder Kenneth Seiff first broke into the e-retailer market in 1991 with Pivot Rules, an online golf apparel store. But in 1998, Seiff's company discontinued its golf sportswear line, sold its Pivot Rules trademarks and made the transition to off-price e-retailer. The new site launched in September 1998, rolling out merchandise that became an immediate hit among label-conscious bargain hunters. An infusion of $10 million in capital from financier George Soros in July 1999 and another $15 million in early 2000 helped Bluefly solidify its standing as a premier online retailer and a legitimate competitor of heavyweights such as Fashionmall.com, Macys.com and Nordstrom.com.

In the red ...

In 2004, Bluefly posted record revenue, boosting sales to $43.8 million from $37.9 million in 2003. The e-retailer also cut costs, improved gross margins and decreased its net loss from $6.4 million in 2003 to $3.8 million in 2004. Still, although the company has shown improvement, Bluefly has yet to turn a profit. Industry experts advise that the crowded retail landscape, flooded with department stores chains, specialty clothing retailers, mass discounters, luxury stores and e-retailers, is bound to slim down soon—through consolidation and closings.

... But not out for the count

So, where does Bluefly sit in the grand scheme of things? A new revolving credit facility of $7.5 million from Wells Fargo (which replaces a $3.5 million credit facility with Rosenthal and Rosenthal) spells good news for the company. So too does the $7 million in gross proceeds the company raised in a private placement in June 2005.

Both will help Bluefly fund a full-scale marketing campaign for the fall of 2005. Bluefly CEO Melissa Payner-Gregor said the firm's primary focus is on increasing its customer base. As of December 2004, the e-retailer has attracted more than 640,000 customers.

GETTING HIRED

Jobs for all

Bluefly posts job openings on its web site, and resumes are accepted via fax or e-mail (jobs@bluefly.com). The e-retailer offers opportunities in a number of areas, including accounting, administrative, business intelligence, customer service, data mining/analysis, design, finance and credit, general admin, human resources, legal, marketing, merchant, online retail, production, public relations, reporting, tech development and tech ops. Prospective hires can search the company's web site by job category or keyword, or simply view all available openings.

Bolt, Inc.

304 Hudson Street, 7th Floor
New York, NY 10013
Phone: (212) 620-5900
Fax: (212) 620-4315
www.bolt.com

LOCATION

New York, NY (HQ)

THE STATS

Employer Type: Private Company
CEO: Aaron Cohen

KEY COMPETITORS

Alloy
IGN Entertainment
mtvU

EMPLOYMENT CONTACT

www.boltinc.com/jobs/index.php

THE SCOOP

Tapping teen trends

Targeting the millions of teens worldwide (not to mention their wallets), Bolt.com has a lofty goal: to become the No.-1 global teen brand. The company has been well on its way to achieving that goal since Dan Pelson founded Bolt in 1997 as part of Concrete Media. Today, the independent Bolt boasts more than 4.5 million registered members, mostly between the ages of 13 and 24. Site features include a daily horoscope, free e-mail, chat rooms, message boards and a Bolt store that sells merchandise.

Teen-authored content

To many teens, Bolt's appeal lies in its authenticity—more than 95 percent of material on the site is written by their peers, not Bolt employees. Pelson views the strategy as a no-brainer: "We empower this audience, and they reward us with loyalty," he says. "They couldn't care less what some 28-year-old [writer] has to say about Eminem or dating. They care what their peers have to say."

The site's channels include Popular Stuff, Movies & TV, Music, Style and News. Users can also communicate via message boards and chat options, post journal entries and photos, join clubs and create "labels" that link to shared interests among members. Bolt members have access to free e-mail and voicemail as well as proprietary tools such as Bolt Notes, a short messaging system, Tagbboks, a "member-created" polling system, and a slew of affiliated teen-friendly web sites featuring buddy icons for AOL Instant Messenger, popular movie quotes, ratings for teachers, gaming tips, creative writing outposts, surveys and an online "living yearbook" for high school students. Faceoffs pit like topics against each other in terms of popularity rating (*Bewitched* the 2005 movie versus *Bewitched* the 1960s television series, for example), and Bolt members can earn "badges" for voting in surveys, posting to boards and frequenting the site.

Advertiser's dream

That authenticity also appeals to advertisers, who get raw feedback on everything from whether McDonald's or Burger King has better hamburgers to whether Jessica Simpson is still hot to what teens are doing on New Year's Eve. And because Bolt's audience is composed of such a wide range of teenagers, advertisers are able to target

Visit Vault at www.vault.com for insider company profiles, expert advice, career message boards, expert resume reviews, the Vault Job Board and more.

VAULT CAREER LIBRARY   45

their ads to specific age groups and localities. (Bolt members must provide their birth date and zip code when registering.) While Bolt doesn't use individual users' real names, advertisers can nonetheless target an ad, for example, to females under 18 living in the Northeast who visited the Unfolding Story section of the site.

Such practices are the bread and butter behind Bolt's business, providing a main source of revenue via sales from advertising and sponsorship, and the sale of demographic information to marketers. Companies also pump new products through the site's "Free Stuff" section, which features contests to win name-brand items like Apple iPods, Saucony sneakers and DVDs of the classic Nickelodeon throwback *Clarissa Explains It All.*

A bolt of fresh air

Co-founders Pelson, Jane Mount and (current CEO) Aaron Cohen cut their teeth during the early 1990s at the online magazine *Word* (another Pelson start-up), and decided to create Bolt as an avenue to connect advertisers with finicky teenagers eschewing "traditional media" in favor of the burgeoning Internet. Early audiences were formed through a 1998 distribution deal with Hotmail, with a focus on both genders—a departure from other up-and-coming rival sites choosing to side with either males or females. Bolt then got a major boost from a February 2000 deal with AOL, which put Bolt in charge of its teen community.

The company shelved a planned IPO in 2000 in favor of a round of financing from venture investors led by Warburg Pincus Ventures, which lent $25 million to the site in order to expand in key areas, add technology and move into new markets in Europe and Asia. At the time, Bolt had over 60,000 members in Britain—its largest concentration outside of North America—and the global numbers were rapidly increasing, with close to a third of the site's audience coming from outside the U.S. In July 2004, Bolt redesigned its web site to enhance advertising capabilities for marketers like Electronic Arts, Verizon Wireless and Old Navy, and to accommodate the millions monthly young visitors flocking to the site.

GETTING HIRED

Hire me!

Bolt lists job openings on its "Hire Me!" web site, www.boltinc.com/jobs/index.php, for a wide range of positions; each posting provides qualification requirements and contact information. The company also has an extensive internship program that allows students to gain experience in most of Bolt's departments.

Visit Vault at **www.vault.com** for insider company profiles, expert advice, career message boards, expert resume reviews, the Vault Job Board and more.

VAULT CAREER LIBRARY   **47**

Broadcom Corporation

16215 Alton Parkway
Irvine, CA 92618-3616
Phone: (949) 450-8700
Fax: (949) 450-8710
www.broadcom.com

LOCATIONS

Irvine, CA (HQ)
Andover, MA • Duluth, GA •
Matawan, NJ • Nashua, NH • San
Diego, CA • San Jose, CA • Santa
Clara, CA • Seattle, WA •
Sunnyvale, CA • Tempe, AZ
40 offices in 15 countries
worldwide.

THE STATS

Employer Type: Public Company
Stock Symbol: BRCM
Stock Exchange: NASDAQ
Chairman: Henry Samueli
CEO: Scott A. McGregor
2004 Employees: 3,373
2004 Revenue ($mil.): $2,400.6

KEY COMPETITORS

Agere Systems
Intel
Texas Instruments

EMPLOYMENT CONTACT

www.broadcom.com/careers

THE SCOOP

Broadly speaking

One of the worldwide leaders in the production of computer chips that power everything from cable boxes to high-speed networks, Broadcom has astounded investors and industry observers alike with its success since its 1991 founding. CEO Henry Nicholas started the company out of his Southern California home after his previous employer, PairGain Technologies, refused to finance a separate unit to develop a new and broader line of technologies. He was soon joined by his former advisor from UCLA's electrical engineering PhD program, Henry Samueli. The company boasted a revenue growth of 5,480 percent between 1994 and 1999, challenging the likes of Intel—a company 50 times its size—and others for supremacy in the highly-competitive realms of chip production and broadband communications. Today, Broadcom's core markets include cable/satellite set-top boxes, gigabit Ethernet, server/storage networks, modems, digital TV, mobile communications, enterprise switching, broadband processors, voice over Internet protocol (VoIP) and network infrastructure. In addition, the company supplies integrated circuits for its digital subscriber line (DSL), carrier access and wireless communications equipment for big-name customers like Hewlett-Packard, Motorola and Dell.

All Broadcom, all the time

Broadcom has also expanded in recent years by spending nearly $1.5 billion to acquire other technology companies. In the summer of 1999, Broadcom bought Hothaus Technologies and AltoCom Inc., both manufacturers of communications software. By mid-2000, Broadcom had also acquired high-tech companies Epigram, Maverick Networks, Armedia, BlueSteel Networks, Digital Furnace, Stellar Semiconductor, Innovent Systems and Pivotal Technologies Corp.

While the company's business is built around its application of computer chip technology, its expansion upon traditional cable and networking offerings gave it a leg up in the high-tech market early on. "Most significant customer" status with LSI Logic Corp. and partnerships with companies like Cisco, Gotcha International (a surfwear and media site targeted at Generation Y), 3Com and TollBridge Technologies helped Broadcom's mission to "connect everyone, everywhere, anytime." The company's aggressive development, including an expansion into fiber-optic networking, quickly secured its position at the vanguard of the chip industry.

Altima, Spice but not everything nice

In August 2000 Broadcom acquired Altima Communications Inc. in a stock deal worth up to $1.15 billion; Altima designed chips used in the small-to-medium business networking market. The deal expanded Brodcom's engineering pool, adding chips that worked inside broadband devices. Analysts suggested that Altima had been having difficulty establishing the global presence it needed to stay competitive.

The same month, the communications-chip maker acquired Silicon Spice Inc. for $1.19 billion in stock. Silicon Spice developed semiconductor technology for voice, fax and data-packet transport. NewPort Communications Inc. also became one of Broadcom's acquisitions for about $1.24 billion in stock. Like Broadcom, was a NewPort developer of high-performance optical-communications chips used in fiber-optic infrastructure.

At the start of 2001, though, over a dozen law firms came out swinging against Broadcom on behalf of purchasers of Broadcom common stock, accusing the company of improper accounting. After a four-year battle, the firm eventually settled with stockholders for $150 million in cash.

Strategy backfires

Overall in 2001, Broadcom surprised the industry by boosting its work force by 12 percent, at a time when rivals were cutting staff. The company took a gamble on the idea that more employees would lead to increased research and development. However, by November 2002, Broadcom was forced to lay off roughly 500 workers and consolidate units to trim down costs amid declining sales. CEO Henry Nicholas quit at the start of 2003, and was replaced by Raju Vegesna, who lasted a mere two months at the top before being asked to step down after a disagreement with the Broadcom board. The turnovers reflected on the boards, forcing stock down as much as 16 percent by March 2003.

Courtroom appeal

While its management played musical chairs, Broadcom also faced battles in the courtroom. In April 2003, radio-frequency chip maker Microtune Inc. won a preliminary injunction barring Broadcom from selling a silicon tuner that allegedly infringed on a Microtune patent. Broadcom announced plans to appeal the ruling, which stemmed from a two-year dispute over patents (the firm later gave Microtune $22.5 million to end litigation). In August 2003, the firm also shelled out $60 million to Intel to settle outstanding patent-related lawsuits. Broadcom finished off the year with a December settlement over—you guessed it—patent infringement with Pctel, a maker of wireless-networking software, worth $3.5 million.

Broadcom once again entered the courts in May 2005, filing a trade complaint against QUALCOMM over patent infringement on chips for mobile phones. A July 2005 lawsuit then accused QUALCOMM of misusing industry standard-setting patents on cellular technology to build a monopoly on cellphone chips. QUALCOMM said the suit was "without merit," and sued Broadcom for patent infringement on seven patents for cellular technology known as CDMA (code-division multiple access). Litigation is pending.

First in line

In the first half of 2004, Broadcom picked up Zyray Wireless and Sand Video Inc. for a total of $175.2 million, adding new semiconductor technology to enhance mobile phones and increase video-transmission volumes, and later settled an outstanding patent lawsuit with Agere Systems for an undisclosed amount that October.

Despite the extended litigation, Broadcom kept its business focus intact, wheeling out a number of industry firsts in 2004, including the first single-chip solution to integrate system requirements for entry-level set-top boxes, the first single-chip, HyperTransport-based server I/O controller for entry-level servers, the first 24-port Fast Ethernet switch, the first single-chip dual-channel high definition video/audio/graphics personal video recorder solution, and the most integrated WiFi router processor of its kind. Such innovations earned Broadcom the title "Most Respected Public Fabless Company" by the Fabless Semiconductor Association. By the end of the year, fourth-quarter revenue and income were up, as the firm recorded its 11th straight period of increasing sales, boosted largely by its expansion into the world of wireless.

Chip off the industry block

At the start of 2005, Scott A. McGregor, a former executive of Royal Philips Electronics, became the firm's president and CEO. Broadcom acquired Siliquent Technologies Inc. for $76 million in July 2005, gaining 10-gigabit Ethernet technology, and also opened a European wireless design center in Denmark. Meanwhile, the firm continues to roll out new technology, including the world's first Bluetooth Enhanced Data Rate (EDR) chip with stereo capabilities, the industry's most advanced HDTV chip supporting both analog and digital reception, and the world's first Gigabit Ethernet IP Phone Chip, which integrates features required for

Visit Vault at www.vault.com for insider company profiles, expert advice, career message boards, expert resume reviews, the Vault Job Board and more.

VAULT CAREER LIBRARY   51

next-generation Internet Protocol phones. Broadcom captured 38 percent of the IP phone chip market in 2004 (the only company to gain market share), and more recently surpassed the 50 million marker for Wi-Fi chipsets shipped, making it the best-selling LAN solution available.

GETTING HIRED

Online offerings

Broadcom lists job openings on its web site, www.broadcom.com/careers. Job seekers can log in, create an account, post a resume and search job offerings for positions around the globe. All positions require an online application.

BroadVision, Inc.

585 Broadway Street
Redwood City, CA 94063
Phone: (650) 542-5100
Fax: (650) 542-5900
www.broadvision.com

LOCATION

Redwood City, CA (HQ)

THE STATS

Employer Type: Public Company
Stock Symbol: BVSN
Stock Exchange: NASDAQ
Chairman & CEO: Pehong Chen
2004 Employees: 337
2004 Revenue ($mil.): $78.0

KEY COMPETITORS

Art Technology Group
Plumtree Software
Vignette

EMPLOYMENT CONTACT

www.broadvision.com/bvsn/bvcom/e
p/browse.do?pageTypeId=8151&ch
annelPage=%2Fjsp%2Fwww%2Fbr
owse%2Fchanneldefault.jsp&channe
lId=-8265&BV_SessionID=NNNN15
90687082.1126213148NNNN&BV_
EngineID=ccccaddehfhhlefcefecefed
ghhdfjl.0

Visit Vault at **www.vault.com** for insider company profiles, expert advice,
career message boards, expert resume reviews, the Vault Job Board and more.

VAULT CAREER LIBRARY

53

THE SCOOP

An e-commerce leader

Redwood City, Calif.-based BroadVision makes Internet commerce easy by providing user-friendly options for companies who want to enter the virtual marketplace. It also allows them to maximize their advertising dollars with specialized consumer tracking technology. A pioneer in e-commerce software, BroadVision licenses its products to businesses for the creation of their commercial web sites and Intranets. The company's highly adaptable "One-to-One" solutions are integrated with existing enterprise systems, allowing companies quick and painless establishment on the Web. Plus, BroadVision's user-friendly interface makes it accessible to the less-than-technologically-oriented user.

Broad range of applications

The One-to-One WebApps suite includes three specific applications: commerce, financial and knowledge management. The most recent version of the software is available in five languages—English, German, Japanese, Chinese and Korean. In addition, the company's One-to-One application records consumer profiles and tracks behavior in order to target advertising and information delivery to individual users. Each visit is tracked in real-time, allowing companies to exploit a direct link to their Internet customers. BroadVision also offers application customization, systems integration, training and consulting services to its customers. The company's list of more than 500 customers in B2B commerce includes Wal-Mart, BT, Home Depot, Nortel, Bell Atlantic, Citibank, Merrill Lynch, British Telecom, American Airlines, Toyota and other big-name clients in the high tech, manufacturing, retail, financial services and telecommunications industries.

Going global

BroadVision's wide range of services has proven attractive to a host of international clients, as well. The company boasts that its applications are available in 120 countries worldwide. BroadVision has seen its influence in foreign markets grow through acquisitions and parnerships. In December 1999 the company announced it would acquire Swiss financial services integration specialists Fidutec Information Technology SA, strengthening the company's presence in Southern and Central European markets. The company later opened sales offices in Milan and Stockholm. In Asia, Broadvision has opened offices in Singapore, Japan, China, Korea and

Taiwan. BroadVision boasts an impressive roster of Asian clients that includes Samsung, Toshiba, China Information Highway Corporation and a host of Asian banks. Finally, the company has established a strong presence in the South American e-commerce market; in 2000 it announced strategic partnerships with Brazilian ASP B2B Inc., eHola.com Inc., and QoS Labs Inc., another ASP starting operations in Florida and Mexico.

Howdy, partner

BroadVision partnered with other businesses in the late 1990s to gain an edge over the competition. To enrich its software offerings, the company teamed up with Internet security specialist VeriSign in April 1998 to incorporate the One-to-One software with VeriSign's digital authentication technology. In 1999, BroadVision inked a $35 million deal with Hewlett-Packard in which HP would sell and help develop BroadVision's business portal software. Also that year, the company signed a deal with Macromedia Inc. making Dreamweaver 2 the exclusive web authoring tool for BroadVision's One-To-One applications. The company then signed software development deals with Novell and Sun Microsystems Inc. In April 2000 BroadVision acquired Interleaf, adding significant wireless technology capabilities to the company's arsenal. And in June 2000, the company teamed up with Madrid-based Amadeus Global Travel Distribution to create a global online travel booking application.

Flying under the radar

In February 2003, the U.S. Air Force began deployment of a BroadVision-powered Air Force Portal, allowing Air Force personnel to log onto computers, check e-mail, get the status of ordered parts and secure other information from anywhere in the world. That August, the firm announced a reseller agreement with International Turnkey Systems, a leading solutions provider with an established presence in the Middle East and Africa. For the fiscal year 2003, BroadVision posted a loss of $35.5 million, a much-needed improvement on the previous year's loss of $170.5 million. Revenue, on the other hand, slipped to $88.1 million from $115.9 million.

In an effort to appease landlords, who were owed $143 million in net future excess real estate obligations, BroadVision established a plan in August 2004 to offer a mix of cash and stock, approximately 2 percent of BroadVision's outstanding shares. CEO Pehong Chen said the arrangement allowed the company to "reduce future

Visit Vault at www.vault.com for insider company profiles, expert advice, career message boards, expert resume reviews, the Vault Job Board and more.

VAULT CAREER LIBRARY   55

facility obligations by 85 percent and move forward with a much improved balance sheet."

Buyout boost

At the start of 2005, BroadVision, facing liquidity challenges, hired a financial advisor to help the company pursue a sale, and eliminated 88 jobs as part of a cost-cutting initiative. That July, Broadcom agreed to be acquired by Vector Capital, a San Francisco-based private equity firm, for $29 million. At the time of the sale, BroadVision had missed three consecutive quarterly revenue targets, and widened its loss margin from $1.5 million the year prior to $2.9 million. The firm will become part of a newly-formed Vector portfolio company that will make it a privately-held, independent software vendor. Vector plans to inject at least $50 million into the company.

GETTING HIRED

Career vision

"Because this company is relatively young," explains one source, "we have had the opportunity to hire very carefully." BroadVision looks for "smart people that can interact with other people and can learn fast." Because they work "on the cutting edge of technology and marketing, we require people that can 'think outside of the box.'" Go to "Jobs at BroadVision" on the company site to find a list of current openings and contact information. Resumes and cover letters may be posted, faxed or e-mailed to hr@broadvision.com. The firm offers jobs in engineering, finance and administration, information technology, marketing, professional services, sales, strategy/business development and support.

OUR SURVEY SAYS

Different: the good and the bad

"The best term to describe the work environment" at BroadVision "is high energy." "You get a chance to create and work with some of the latest in Internet technology" as well as "some of the biggest companies and prominent figures in the information technology industry." Employees of this "rapidly growing company" are proud to note that BroadVision is "one of the few Internet companies to actually turn profitable." Insiders say the best part of working at BroadVision is the wide variety of customers they serve. "We are always getting contracts for things that we've never done before. This keeps the job fun, because you never do the same thing twice."

Be prepared though, sources note that this can sometimes be "a bit frustrating," and several insiders say they are "always trying to play catch-up on learning the technology." "I probably spend several hundred dollars a year on books," reported one source, "just to keep up with the ever-changing world of the Internet." "For the most part this place has been fun every single day," said a source who has "been with the company from the start." "Your work counts," adds another insider, "certainly within BroadVision but also in the web industry."

Social dogs

"Although we went public over two years ago," one insider notes, "we have tried to keep all of the good qualities of a start-up." He went on to say that "though in the beginning we worked a gazillion hours," they managed to develop "a really good social atmosphere." As the company grew, "we tried to keep the cultural aspects of the company while not making everyone work the gazillion hours." "We even have an employee whose full-time job is to plan employee events, like our weekly happy hour (the company foots the bill) and our summer picnics." The company also provides "a rec room with a pool table and satellite TV," plus free sodas and junk food. If you're into more high-powered de-stressing, "we have locker rooms and showers if you want to work out during the day." Employees are allowed to bring their dogs to work, so "every so often you might have one wander into your office." Salaries are "commensurate with the rest of the Silicon Valley area." Those in the engineering department look forward to "cash bonuses for making deliver schedules," while outstanding sales people get free vacations.

Hours

In general, BroadVision is a "very friendly environment," where "there is no dress code" for employees who "deal only internally." Sales and consulting people "wear suits on the days we interact with customers." Most employees wear jeans to the office, and "it's not uncommon to see people barefoot." Just pray their toes are clean. "There are no set hours for work," but people should be in the office "between the hours of 10 a.m. to 4 p.m., so that everyone is in the office for group meetings." At

Visit Vault at **www.vault.com** for insider company profiles, expert advice, career message boards, expert resume reviews, the Vault Job Board and more.

VAULT CAREER LIBRARY

57

BroadVision, "the emphasis is on results." Most people arrive after 9 a.m. and stay until 7 or 8 at night, and "most people don't work weekends." In addition, "no one says anything if people prefer to work at home, provided they make all mandatory meetings and are approachable when they're not at the office."

Women? Yes. Minorities? Mixed.

Women and minorities interested in working at BroadVision will be happy to learn that "the company has many women holding positions across the board up and down the hierarchy." Though there was one strange comment from an insider at the company's HQ: "we have only two black employees (out of a total of 200+), but they are highly regarded." Nevertheless, even female employees insist that "there is no glass ceiling," and "discrimination of any sort is out of the question" in this "diversified" and "results-oriented" company.

Buy.com

85 Enterprise, Suite 100
Aliso Viejo, CA 92656
Phone: (949) 389-2000
Fax: (949) 389-2800
www.buy.com

LOCATION

Aliso Viejo, CA (HQ)

THE STATS

Employer Type: Private Company
Chairman & CEO: Scott A. Blum
2004 Employees: 121
2004 Revenue ($mil.): $290.8

KEY COMPETITORS

Amazon.com
Best Buy
Circuit City

EMPLOYMENT CONTACT

www.buy.com/toc/Job_Opportunities
/15795.html

Visit Vault at **www.vault.com** for insider company profiles, expert advice,
career message boards, expert resume reviews, the Vault Job Board and more.

VAULT CAREER LIBRARY   **59**

THE SCOOP

One stop shopping

When Buy.com bills itself as "The Internet Superstore," it's hard to argue: the web site sells books, cell phones, computer hardware and software, electronics, DVDs, music, and toys—overall, more than 2 million products. The company made a name for itself in the late 1990s by selling products below cost; today, prices have been raised but remain competitive. Buy.com also distributes *BuyMagazine*, a monthly digital publication featuring product reviews, to its 7 million customers. *Internet Retailer* named the site to its Top 50 web sites in 2002 and 2003, and has earned the praises of *PC Magazine*, *Forbes* and BizRate.com.

Blum's comings and goings

Founder Scott Blum first established the company in 1997 under the moniker BUYCOMP.com as the Internet hit the public full speed. By February 1998, the site eclipsed 1 million hits in a single day, driven by a catalog of over 30,000 tech products. That November, the firm shortened its name to Buy.com, and set a first-year record of $125 million the following month. A year later, Blum sold the company to Japanese investment firm Softbank for $230 million, just as Buy.com first filed to go public. Stock skyrocketed 93 percent before succumbing to the dot-com bust that paralyzed many tech firms at the start of the 21st century. By February 2001, Buy.com stock had slipped more than 97 percent, forcing then-CEO Gregory Hawkins to resign. Blum stepped up to the plate, reacquired the firm from Softbank for a bargain $26 million, and took it private.

Pixels and paper to the rescue

To boost its bottom line in 2001, Buy.com laid off 80 percent of its workforce, sold its U.K. operation, discontinued a joint venture in Australia and shut down its Canadian web site. To earn additional sales, Buy.com began producing its quarterly merchandise magazine in the spring of 2002, part of a "pixels and paper strategy" engineered by Blum that focused on helping consumers make better buying decisions. Rival Amazon.com challenged Buy.com's strategy of free shipping with its own free promotion during the summer of 2002, leading analysts to assume the latter was locked in an uphill battle against the larger Amazon. Undaunted, Buy.com took on another major Internet retailer the following year. Its BuyMusic.com site, which offered a legal way to download music, came in direct competition with the mighty

Apple iTunes store in July 2003. Overall in 2003, Nielsen/NetRatings ranked Buy.com No. 3 among fastest growing retail web sites—and with good reason. The firm opened a sports store and toy store by the year's close, and a cellular store at the start of 2004.

Second time's the charm?

In January 2005, Buy.com filed for a second IPO as part of a plan to raise $83.2 million for technology and systems upgrades, as well as sales and marketing activities. However, analysts were skeptical of the firm's stock the second time around, especially since Buy.com has never turned a profit during its eight years of existence and has seen revenue slip from $787.6 million in 2000 to $290.7 million in 2004, while competitors like Overstock.com continue to rise in profits.

GETTING HIRED

Monster opportunities

Buy.com posts job openings on Monster.com at jobsearch.buy.com.careers. monster.com. Through Monster.com, job seekers can also establish an account, upload a resume and create a profile.

Visit Vault at **www.vault.com** for insider company profiles, expert advice, career message boards, expert resume reviews, the Vault Job Board and more.

VAULT CAREER LIBRARY

61

CDC Corporation

34/F Citicorp Centre
18 Whitfield Rd., Causeway Bay
Hong Kong
Phone: +852-2893-8200
Fax: +852-2893-5245
www.cdccorporation.net

LOCATIONS

Hong Kong (HQ)
New York, NY

THE STATS

Employer Type: Public Company
Stock Symbol: CHINA
Stock Exchange: NASDAQ
Chairman: Dr. Raymond Ch'ien
Acting CEO: Steven Chan
2004 Employees: 1,802
2004 Revenue ($mil.): $182.7

KEY COMPETITORS

Infosys
Oracle
SAP

EMPLOYMENT CONTACT

E-mail inquiries:
contact@cdccorporation.net

THE SCOOP

Wiring the non-Western world

The first Hong Kong-based Internet company to be listed on Nasdaq, CDC Corporation (formerly chinadotcom corporation) had high aspirations: not only to be the primary pan-Asian web portal, but also to help jumpstart the Internet economy in Asia by providing seed money, web design and e-commerce services to Asian e-startups. CDC's first incarnation was as the China Internet Corp., established by computer scientist (and Hong Kong native) James Chu in 1994. By partnering with Xinhua News Agency, the state-run Chinese media outlet, Chu shrewdly guaranteed his company implicit government sanction—a move particularly important in a country intent on maintaining tight control over the flow of information from the Internet to its citizens. In recent years, though, the company has moved away from an Internet portal model and has found success as a software and technology services firm, offering application integration, software development, e-business consulting, online advertising and media planning.

The total package

The corporation provides software solutions for mid-sized companies through five major subsidiaries: CDC Software Asia Pacific, Platinum China, Industri-Matematik, Pivotal, and Ross Systems. Among the services provided are enterprise resource planning, customer relationship management, supply chain management, order management systems, human resources, payroll management and business intelligence. Through its enterprise software unit, CDC accommodates 3,500 customers worldwide. Business services cover Hong Kong, Australia, Korea and the U.S., while the mobile applications market is focused on China. CDC also offers online entertainment and Internet services to users in China through its portal networks, www.china.com and www.hongkong.com, and owns a number of technology services and outsourcing firms, including Ion Global, PK Information Systems and Praxa.

WTO membership a boon

In November 1999, China's entrance into the World Trade Organization meant new opportunities for CDC. Before that time, foreign companies were only allowed to own a small stake in Chinese telecommunications and Internet companies. The agreement, however, stipulated that foreign companies could own up to 50 percent of

Chinese e-companies, sending CDC's stock skyrocketing. Rumors that America Online, already a 10 percent owner, was interested in purchasing a greater share further boosted the company's profile.

In December 1999, CEO Peter Yip announced that CDC had invested $10 million in a program to help small- and mid-sized companies start e-businesses, an example of one of three investment strategies practiced by the corporation; other strategies included acceleration to speed the growth of existing online services, partnership with already established Internet companies and incubation of Internet start-ups. In April 2003, the company began paid e-mail services to boost its bottom line, and launched a wireless platform through a joint venture with Nokia to promote mobile services in Mainland China. Third quarter profit posted that November reported a 103 percent year-on-year growth in revenue to $24.4 million. To expand further, CDC made a move to acquire Pivotal Corp., though the bid was rejected. CDC, wasting no time, picked up Ross Systems, a developer of enterprise management software, instead. However, by the end of 2003, Pivotal agreed to be acquired by CDC, thus boosting the latter's CRM software capabilities.

Change is underway

The buying game hit the company hard in March 2005, after CDC revealed a widening fourth-quarter loss margin due to acquisitions-related tax expenses. CEO Yip announced his resignation the same month. As part of a rebranding strategy to move its image away from its former Internet focus, the company changed its name from chinadotcom to CDC Corporation in April 2005. Restructuring continued that summer, as CDC announced a number of executive management team changes that saw Steven Chan, the company's general counsel, take over the CEO role on an interim basis as the board searched for a replacement for Yip. Chief Financial Officer Keith Oliver also announced his resignation effective October 2005. He was replaced by Vincent Leung

GETTING HIRED

The great unknown

There is no career information available on the web site, and the New York City office appears to just house investor relations. But the site does provide a general e-mail address for queries, so interested applicants should send a query to contact@cdccorporation.net.

Visit Vault at **www.vault.com** for insider company profiles, expert advice,
career message boards, expert resume reviews, the Vault Job Board and more.

VAULT CAREER LIBRARY

65

CNET Networks, Inc.

235 Second Street
San Francisco, CA 94105
Phone: (415) 344-2000
Fax: (415) 395-9207
www.cnetnetworks.com

LOCATIONS

San Francisco, CA (HQ)
Bridgewater, NJ • Cambridge, MA •
Chicago, IL • Irvine, CA • Los
Angeles, CA • Louisville, KY • New
York, NY • Beijing • London • Paris •
Moscow • Munich • St. Légier,
Switzerland • Seoul • Singapore •
Sydney • Taipei • Tokyo

THE STATS

Employer Type: Public Company
Stock Symbol: CNET
Stock Exchange: NASDAQ
Chairman & CEO: Shelby W. Bonnie
2004 Employees: 2,080
2004 Revenue ($mil.): $291.2

KEY COMPETITORS

CMP Media
IGN Entertainment
Shopping.com

EMPLOYMENT CONTACT

www.cnetnetworks.com/careers

THE SCOOP

Keeping the tech world informed

CNET keeps the world abreast of the most important developments in the world of computers and cyberspace, and is one of the few companies that publishes original content on the Internet. Halsey Minor founded CNET in 1992 with $5 million in venture capital from Microsoft co-founder Paul Allen. Intel owns a 5 percent stake in the company. Minor's intent was to develop a cable network devoted to computers and new technology, with a companion project on the Internet. In April 1995 it launched a weekly half-hour program on the USA Network, and cnet.com, featuring news, product reviews and helpful tips. Today CNET has several Internet sites devoted to topics ranging from computer and technology news to web design, from online gaming to downloadable software, including the web sites ZDNet and Computer Shopper, as well as CNET Download.com (freeware and shareware software), BNET (technology and business news), Webshots (photo sharing), GameSpot (video game-related content), MP3.com (digital music information), and mySimon (price comparison shopping).

CNET's brightly-colored, user-friendly sites consistently snag the best ratings in their category, and have evolved into a high-tech staple. Those in the business trust it to provide up-to-the-minute information, and those in the know look to CNET's product reviews before they buy. It's no surprise, then, that advertisers love CNET's sites, as they have become the standard for tech professionals.

Shopping and name-dropping

In March 2000, CNET also acquired online shopping site mySimon.com, and changed its own corporate name to CNET Networks, Inc. to reflect the inclusion of the various sites and services it now offers. The move was made in order to transform CNET into the "Internet's number one comparison shopping resource for computer and consumer electronics products." The same month, CNET founder Halsey Minor stepped down from the firm, replaced by Vice Chairman Shelby Bonnie. Bonnie, a CNET veteran with seven years' experience at the firm, was CNET's first major investor as a managing director for Tiger Management in the early 1990s.

Boosting its business-to-business e-commerce offerings, CNET acquired Apollo Solutions Inc. in July 2000 for $11.2 million in stock and cash. Apollo provides web-based applications that allow computer product resellers to obtain product information from manufacturers.

All over the world

Adding global reach across 25 countries in Europe, Asia, North America and Latin America to the technology information company, CNET acquired ZDNet from Ziff-Davis in July 2000 for $1.6 billion in stock, along with Ziff-Davis' *Computer Shopper*, a computer buyer guide, and web site Smart Planet, an online educational service focused on the technology industry. CNET chief exec Shelby Bonnie remained CEO of the combined entity, which logged 1,600 employees and more than $500 million in revenue in 2001.

Focus on content

In April 2001, CNET acquired TechRepublic Inc., an online reference site designed for IT professionals, for $23 million in cash and stock. In June 2002, the company announced it was cutting staff by roughly 10 percent, lowering revenue forecasts, and realigning itself around six business categories (business technology, commerce, downloads, gaming, international and channel) as part of a restructuring plan to "focus on enhancing service to the unique user, marketer and industry customers within each category."

By March 2004, the firm had announced plans to purchase EDventure Holdings, Inc. for an undisclosed amount, adding EDventure's monthly technology reports and annual technology conferences to its holdings. That July, CNET picked up Twofold Photos, owner of the popular Webshots photography web site, for $70 million. Next up was the October 2004 acquisition of ZOL and Fengniao, two Chinese web sites focusing on online personal technology-related content, and digital camera and photography content, respectively. For all of its wheeling and dealing, the company posted a net income of $11.7 million on revenue of $291.2 million in 2004. CEO Bonnie praised the company for achieving "growth objectives," and looked forward to a strong performance in 2005, centered on an ongoing focus on content innovation and expansion.

Reaching out to new customers

As part of a plan to gain more business from businesses, CNET launched Bnet.com in April 2005, a B2B venture featuring whitepapers, case studies, webcasts, audiocasts, targeted e-mail alerts, newsletters, RSS feeds and business-related blogs.

The same month, CNET acquired Windup Labs and its HeyPix! online photo service for an undisclosed amount, strengthening its online photo services, and also Shanghai-based PCHome for $11 million, in an effort to expand its holdings and online presence in the fast growing Chinese markets.

More recent ventures include the June 2005 launch of TV.com, an online destination for TV fans with information on more than 2,500 series from the 1940s to current favorites like *Desperate Housewives* and *24*. CNET built the new site from its previous acquisition of TVTome, a user-drive content site acquired in January 2005. The same summer, CNET purchased Metacritic Inc., a Santa Monica, Calif.-based web site providing reviews of films, books, games and music. The new acquisitions enhance the firm's demographic reach, including more exposure to the female market, and allow for the opportunity to work with a wider range of advertisers.

GETTING HIRED

Networking

CNET, which bills itself as "a different kind of media company," wants employees with a real love for technology and the possibilities of the Internet. Visit the company web site at www.cnetnetworks.com/careers for a list of current job opportunities sorted by department and location.

OUR SURVEY SAYS

A smart but loaded office

The work environment at CNET is "very young and relaxed" and the company's employees are "some of the smartest people you could ever meet." Insiders describe it as "very diverse," adding that "we have a large percentage of women and minorities all the way to upper management." Be careful what you say around the office, though—one source reveals that several employees have problems with superiors. Another insider reports that "a few careers have been killed by politics through e-mail."

Visit Vault at **www.vault.com** for insider company profiles, expert advice, career message boards, expert resume reviews, the Vault Job Board and more.

VAULT CAREER LIBRARY

69

Manage your time to earn the bucks

Perks and benefits "are typical for Silicon Valley," notes a source who cites "hard work, flex-time and competitive pay." The dress code "is business casual, but upper management seems to dress a bit more formally." In most departments, typical hours are 9 a.m. to 6:30 p.m. However, people in tech positions usually work 50- to 70-hour weeks. Employees enjoy typical high-tech salaries and "all the usual benefits—401(k), stock options and so on."

craigslist, inc.

1381 9th Avenue
San Francisco, CA 94122-2308
Phone: (415) 566-6394
Fax: (415) 504-6394
www.craigslist.org

LOCATION

San Francisco, CA (HQ)

Visit Vault at **www.vault.com** for insider company profiles, expert advice,
career message boards, expert resume reviews, the Vault Job Board and more.

VAULT CAREER LIBRARY

71

THE SCOOP

Name in the know

Self-proclaimed nerd Craig Newmark can thank a bit of HTML code and a small gesture of Bay Area good will for his becoming one of the most talked about names across towns. From San Francisco to New York City, Amsterdam to Zurich, Bangalore to Johannesburg—Newmark's brainchild, a community bulletin board aptly named "craigslist," is sweeping the globe. Craigslist serves 175 cities in all 50 states and 35 countries (offering descriptions of each place via a Wikipedia link). Postings run the gamut from ride shares to vacation rentals to legal services, and even "missed connections" for the fated soul mates who exchange glances across the subway platform. Jobs, housing and sale listings are the most popular.

The little site that could maintains a set of impressive ambitions, including the simple mission of "getting the word out about everyday, real-world stuff" to the more complex—"restoring the human voice to the Internet"—and even quasi-political— "giving a voice to the disenfranchised." No matter what web surfers are seeking, though, one thing is clear: they flock to craigslist in droves. On a monthly basis, the site logs over 3 billion page views, attracts 10 million users, lists more than 5 million classified ads and hosts 1 million forum postings.

A modest proposal

Newmark began his now-legendary list as a listserv in 1995 to provide a way to publicize events around his San Francisco digs to friends. They demanded more listings; he launched a web site, craigslist.org, to accommodate his growing fan base. Craigslist quietly rode the Internet rise and fall, survived the dot-com bust and continued to grow. In 1997, Newmark made the executive decision to ban banner ads from the site after being approached by marketing firms, declaring, "Some things should be about money, some shouldn't." He quit a contract programming job to run craigslist full time in 1999, the same year the bustling business became profitable.

Jim Buckmaster signed on as CEO in 2000, while Newmark retained the position of chairman (though he doesn't use that title anymore, opting instead for customer service rep and founder). eBay purchased a 25 percent stake in the firm in August 2004, citing craigslist as "an excellent example of how the Internet brings people together." Newmark and co. look to use the partnership with the successful auctioneer to improve craigslist's user accessibility and to combat increasing attacks from hackers and spammers.

Press picks and pans

In the meantime, the company has been recognized by a slew of media outposts, and been named to a number of "best" lists, including "Best eBay Alternative" (*New York Press*), "Best Resource for Finding Just About Anything" (*San Francisco Bay Guardian*), "50 Coolest Websites" (*Time* magazine), and #1 Most Efficient U.S. Job Site (*The Wall Street Journal*). Filmmaker Michael Ferris Gibson even created an independent film, *24 Hours on Craigslist.org*, which debuted at the 2004 South by Southwest festival.

Not everyone is a fan, though—newspapers in major craigslist markets have lost millions in merchandise, real estate and classified advertising as a result of craigslist's cheaper posting capabilities. Craigslist says the lost revenue is highly disputed as its clientele is comprised mainly of advertisers who can't afford ad placement in larger newspapers, or whose ads would not fit most shortened newspaper listing formats.

It's not about the money

The company's staff of 18 is housed in San Francisco, and business is supported by charging a $75 fee in San Francisco, and a $25 fee in New York and Los Angeles, to post job openings; all other postings are free. Craigslist is currently mulling charging for help wanted ads in Boston, its fourth-largest market, and possibly tacking a price tag onto New York apartment listings. "Everyone else can make as much as they want," Newmark explains of his uncharacteristically charitable business. "But nerd values suggest you live comfortably—then try to change the world."

GETTING HIRED

Gut your name on the list

Craislist posts openings in its office in the jobs section of its San Francisco Bay area site. To get more information, call the main number or click on the "contact us" link and fill out the form to send a query.

Delphi Forums LLC

25 Porter Road
Littleton, MA 01460
Phone: (978) 698-6599
Fax: (978) 698-6515
www.delphiforums.com

LOCATION

Littleton, MA (HQ)

THE STATS

Employer Type: Subsidiary of
Prospero Technologies
General Manager: Dawn Ferragamo

KEY COMPETITORS

Friendster
MySpace.com
Meetup.com

EMPLOYMENT CONTACT

www.delphiforums.com/jobs.htm

THE SCOOP

A forum for growth

Delphi Forums, formerly Delphi, traces its roots back to 1983 when it was founded as a consumer online service. The company is responsible for online innovations such as real-time chat, online auctions and online communities. Today, Delphi Forums houses two web sites, Delphi Forums and Talk City, both geared toward enabling individuals to build, manage and grow their own online communities. Together, the sites boast more than 10 million registered users and more than one million new messages posted per week. The company is a subsidiary of Prospero Technologies, formed in January 2000 as a result of the merger of Delphi Forums and Well Engaged, the software and business services spin-off from The Well, one of the earliest online communities.

The basic membership to Delphi Forums is free and includes access to the site's more than 8,000 active forums, such as "Etiquette Hell," "About to Crack" and "Preparing for Pregnancy." Delphi affiliates can also chat online and create their own personalized forum. For a fee, members can up their status to DelphiPlus or DelphiAdvanced, plans which allow users to browse forums ad-free, include special fonts and colors in messages, or create a personal icon.

Talk City, Delphi's other online community site, offers users three different membership options: Starter, Talk Citizen Basic and Talk Citizen Owner. The starter membership allows members to explore the site's chat rooms and message boards before committing to Talk Citizenship. Basic Talk Citizens get access to preferred customer support and advanced chat options via Internet Relay Chat software, while Talk Citizen Owners have the opportunity to create their own chat room and message board. The site also boasts online games such as Alphabet Soup, Finders Keepers and Ridiculist.

GETTING HIRED

The job forum

Individuals interested in working for Delphi Forums should check out the list of current opportunities on the company's careers page (www.delphiforums.com

Visit Vault at **www.vault.com** for insider company profiles, expert advice, career message boards, expert resume reviews, the Vault Job Board and more.

VAULT CAREER LIBRARY

75

jobs.htm). The company offers an "informal, collaborative office atmosphere" and a complete benefits package.

Dice Inc.

3 Park Avenue, 33rd Floor
New York, NY 10016
Phone: (212) 725-6550
Fax: (212) 725-6559
www.dice.com

LOCATIONS

New York, NY (HQ)
Urbandale, IA
Alpharetta, GA
Cincinnati, OH

WEBSITES

ClearanceJobs.com
Dice.com
Measureup.com
TargetedJobFairs.com

THE STATS

Employer Type: Private Company
President and CEO: Scot W. Melland
2004 Employees: Approx. 150

KEY COMPETITORS

CareerBuilder
Monster
Techies.com

EMPLOYMENT CONTACT

Dice Human Resources
4101 NW Urbandale Drive
Urbandale, IA 50322
Fax: (515) 313-2347
E-mail: HR@dice.com

Visit Vault at **www.vault.com** for insider company profiles, expert advice,
career message boards, expert resume reviews, the Vault Job Board and more.

VAULT CAREER LIBRARY   77

THE SCOOP

A roll of the dice

Dice Inc., best known for its eponymous web site, was founded in 1991, before the dot-com start-up boom era and met with early success as the tech-centered career development company. Dice was purchased by EarthWeb in 1999. EarthWeb bolstered its position in the IT world in the late 1990s and the turn of the century through a series of acquisitions, including MeasureUp.com, an online certification prep and assessment company for the IT industry. At its peak, EarthWeb operated more than a dozen web sites and newsletters.

Despite the fact that Dice and MeasureUp were always profitable, the company filed for bankruptcy under Chapter 11 in February 2003, which the company says was basically a recapitalization. EarthWeb had issued a large amount of debt in 2000 that resulted in an unstable cororate structure. By the end of June 2003, Dice came out of bankruptcy, eliminating $69.4 million worth of debt and going through the change from public company to private. More recently, in August 2005, Dice underwent yet another change: two private equity firms, General Atlantic LLC and Quadrangle Group LLC, acquired it from the previous private investor owners. Dice says that its relationship with EarthWeb "has no real impact on the current state of the company."

"Essentially, it was a relatively healthy business that had a bad capital structure," Dice President and CEO Scott Melland said of the bankrupcy. "The good news, coming out of the other side of it, is that we had no debt, and we could take what we were paying in interest payments and put it into building the business."

Dice anew

Dice emerged from bankruptcy with positive cash flow and enough cash to invest in its own rebuilding. At the time, Dice operated just two web sites, Dice.com, the leading online job board used by IT professionals providing job postings, career tools, salary surveys and career links, and MeasureUp.com. In September 2004, Dice acquired ClearanceJobs.com, a job board focused on candidates with active U.S. government security clearance; and in January 2005, Dice bought up TargetedJobFairs.com, which provides information on career fairs and is also targeted toward individuals with security clearance.

Dice also blazed a path into the engineering job sector in a move to diversify its client base and expand into new markets in July 2004. "We have Fortune 500 and Fortune

100 customers," Melland said in an interview with *Business Record.* "Whereas before, many of our clients were mom-and-pop recruiters who went out of business."

GETTING HIRED

A drive for tech

Want a job at Dice? The company encourages people with technical and creative ability to send a resume to HR@dice.com. For a list of current openings, candidates should check out the jobs section at the bottom of the company's web site (see "Jobs at Dice"). Postings include a list of essential functions, additional responsibilities and minimum qualifications. Dice promises its employees a "high-tech work environment" with a competitive salary and comprehensive benefits package.

Visit Vault at **www.vault.com** for insider company profiles, expert advice,
career message boards, expert resume reviews, the Vault Job Board and more.

V∧ULT CAREER LIBRARY   79

Digitas Inc.

Prudential Tower
800 Boylston Street
Boston, MA 02199
Phone: (617) 867-1000
Fax: (617) 867-1111
www.digitasinc.com

LOCATIONS

Boston, MA (HQ)
Chicago, IL
New York, NY
Norwalk, CT
San Francisco, CA
London

DEPARTMENTS

Digitas
Modem Media

THE STATS

Employer Type: Public Company
Stock Symbol: DTAS
Stock Exchange: NASDAQ
Chairman and CEO: David W. Kenny
2004 Employees: 1,500
2004 Revenue ($mil.): $382.0
million

KEY COMPETITORS

aQuantive
Agency.com

EMPLOYMENT CONTACT

Apply online via www.digitas.com or
www.modemmedia.com.

THE SCOOP

From traditional to digital

Digitas traces its roots back to 1980, when the direct marketing firm was known as Bronner Slosberg Humphrey. Over the years, the company added telemarketing and Internet marketing to its areas of expertise and went through a number of name changes, morphing from Bronnercom to Strategic Interactive Group and, finally, to Digitas. Today, Digitas is one of two agencies under the umbrella of Digitas Inc. Digitas' sister company, Modem Media, was acquired in July 2004. Digitas has offices in Boston, Chicago and New York City; Modem Media has outposts in San Francisco, London and Norwalk, Connecticut. Together, the two agencies boast some 1,500 employees and a client list that includes General Motors, American Express and AT&T.

A tale of two agencies

Digitas breaks its business down into two main areas, marketing strategy and enablement, and marketing agency services. The marketing strategy and enablement segment works with clients to lay the strategy and technology foundation for companies just starting to build marketing engines, discover new growth strategies and optimize budget and programs for the best possible return. Marketing agency services include communications strategy, program development and campaign execution across a range of channels—digital marketing, Internet solutions, live channels, promotions and traditional direct response.

Modern Media divides its expertise into three segments: planning and management, executive, and higher level program design. Founded in 1987, the newcomer to the Digitas family, is known for a number of online innovations. Modem Media built the first online shopping environment, pioneered the integration of e-commerce with existing database systems and built the first consumer-product web site. The company also built the first White House site in 1995.

Visit Vault at **www.vault.com** for insider company profiles, expert advice, career message boards, expert resume reviews, the Vault Job Board and more.

VAULT CAREER LIBRARY   81

GETTING HIRED

On the employment front

Digitas Inc. offers career opportunities for "online and offline creative types, operations gurus, promotions experts, marketing strategists, technologists and global support staff." Candidates should check out the career pages at each of the company's subsidiary web sites, www.digitas.com and www.modemmedia.com.

Insiders report that the employees work hard but are well compensated. Furthermore, one source notes that Digitas "is not a design-friendly place, though it doesn't really pretend to be." On a more positive note, Digitas was listed as one of the best places to work by the *Boston Business Journal* in 2004 and 2005.

Dimension Data Holdings plc

110 Parkway Drive South
Hauppauge, NY 11788
Phone: (631) 543-6100
www.dimensiondata.com

LOCATIONS

Hauppauge, NY (US HQ)
Additional offices in 30 countries.

SUBSIDIARIES

Datacraft
Merchants
Internet Solutions

THE STATS

Employer Type: Public Company
Stock Symbol: DDT
Stock Exchange: LSE
Chairman: Jeremy J. Ord
CEO: Brett W. Dawson
2004 Employees: 8,563
2004 Revenue (£mil): 1,380.4

KEY COMPETITORS

Accenture
EDS
IBM Global Services

EMPLOYMENT CONTACT

www.dimensiondata.com/AboutUs/
Careers/CareersOverview.htm

Visit Vault at **www.vault.com** for insider company profiles, expert advice,
career message boards, expert resume reviews, the Vault Job Board and more.

VAULT CAREER LIBRARY

83

THE SCOOP

South Africa and beyond

Founded in 1983, Dimension Data Holdings has come a long way since its humble beginnings. Today, it is South Africa's largest information technology company. DiData also boasts a significant international reach, with outposts in 30 countries on six continents. In the United States, the South African company has 11 offices, with headquarters in Hauppauge, New York. DiData's global presence is bolstered by its three subsidiaries, Singapore-based Datacraft, Merchants, headquartered in the U.K., and Internet Solutions, South Africa's largest ISP.

DiData helps clients design, build and maintain their IT infrastructures. Its services fall into three main areas: professional services, which include consulting and technology integration; managed services, which involve support and monitoring; and IT procurement. The firm's solutions run the gamut from network integration and security to operating environment and messaging. DiData serves a number of industries, with a focus on financial services, government, health care and manufacturing.

Black empowerment

In September 2004, DiData announced a black economic empowerment (BEE) deal which was hailed as one of the most profound in the sector. The transaction included black investors taking a 25 percent stake in Dimension Data. The consortium, comprised of Ngcaba Holdings, Safika Holdings and various empowerment groups and staff, was given full voting rights and the ability to appoint three directors to the board. The BEE partners are locked in until 2009.

GETTING HIRED

Check'em out

Interested individuals should check out the career section of DiData's web site, www.dimensiondata.com, which includes information on life at the company, job functions, training and development, and current job opportunities.

drugstore.com, inc.

411 108th Avenue NW
Suite 1400
Bellevue, WA 98004
Phone: (425) 372-3200
Fax: (425) 372-3800
www.drugstore.com

LOCATIONS

Bellevue, WA (HQ)
Bridgeport, NJ
Halifax, Nova Scotia

THE STATS

Employer Type: Public Company
Stock Symbol: DSCM
Stock Exchange: NASDAQ
Chairman, President and CEO: Dawn G. Lepore
2004 Employees: 664
2004 Revenue ($mil.): $360.1

KEY COMPETITORS

CVS
Walgreen
Wal-Mart

EMPLOYMENT CONTACT

E-mail: jobs@drugstore.com

Visit Vault at **www.vault.com** for insider company profiles, expert advice, career message boards, expert resume reviews, the Vault Job Board and more.

VAULT CAREER LIBRARY   85

THE SCOOP

Bubble bath to birth control

With thousands of products—from bubble bath to birth control—drugstore.com is changing the way Americans shop for personal care items by shipping everything to their doors. Since its beginnings in 1998, the e-retailer has significantly expanded its product offerings, which now run the gamut from household items to homeopathic health supplements, from cough medicine to contact lenses. The launch of the boutique section in late 1999, with high-end brands like Philosophy, Ahava, Zirh and Peter Thomas Roth Clinical Skincare, signaled drugstore.com's eagerness to reach out to a more upscale customer. The acquisition of Beauty.com, a posh purveyor of makeup, skin care and fragrances, in January 2000 for $42 million in stock also helped solidify the company's up-market strategy.

In addition to a plethora of brand-name personal health care, beauty and wellness items, the site offers a full-service, licensed retail pharmacy that gives users the option of having orders delivered (new orders take about 14 days; refills take six to eight days) or picking up prescriptions at any one of 3,600 RiteAid stores nationwide. Customers can also find out about safety concerns through the site's eMedAlert program or access drug interaction information online. The Ask Your Pharmacist feature allows consumers to question drugstore.com pharmacists about OTC and wellness products as well as prescription drugs.

Still losing money, but ...

In a decade when Internet companies are dropping like flies (witness the failure of competitor PlanetRx), drugstore.com has staged an impressive turnaround. The e-retailer saw its stock climb from 46 cents in 2001 to around $2.86 as of January 2006. The online drugstore also saw sales more than triple from $110 million in 2001 to $360 million in 2004. Still, the company continues to lose money. So, why are industry experts still optimistic? One good reason is the appointment of Dawn Lepore as the company's chairman and CEO in September 2004. The former Charles Schwab vice chair is a board member of both Wal-Mart and eBay. In other words, the seasoned executive has knowledge of both traditional retailing and online e-commerce. More recently, the drug and beauty product e-retailer added four more veterans to its senior management team: John Tinter, vice president, business strategy; Matthew Septka, vice president, pharmacy; Talat Sadiq, chief information officer; and John Helm, chief technology officer. Lepore said she believes the new team has the "right stuff" to take drugstore.com to the next level—profitability.

A feather in Lepore's cap, drugstore.com recently reached a number of operational milestones. In February 2005, the company announced that it had achieved lifetime revenues of $1 billion, shipped 10 million OTC packages, fulfilled 3 million prescriptions and its customer base had reached 6 million.

GETTING HIRED

Jobs

Individuals interested in working for drugstore.com can search the list of current job opportunities on firm's web site (see "employment" at the bottom of the screen). Jobs are broken down by location—the company has offices in Bellevue, Washington, Bridgeport, New Jersey and Halifax, Nova Scotia—and each location is further broken down by area of interest. For example, job seekers in Bellevue may find a career in design, editorial, finance and administration, marketing, merchandising, system and network operations or web site development and production. Candidates who find a position they are interested in should e-mail their resume to jobs@drugsore.com.

Drugstore.com also participates in campus recruiting. As of January 2006, there are no openings available from campus recruiting, but check back at the site for further information.

Visit Vault at **www.vault.com** for insider company profiles, expert advice, career message boards, expert resume reviews, the Vault Job Board and more.

V/\ULT CAREER LIBRARY   87

EarthLink, Inc.

1375 Peachtree Street, Level A
Atlanta, GA 30309
Phone: (404) 815-0770
Fax: (404) 892-7616
www.earthlink.net

LOCATIONS

Atlanta, GA (HQ)
Harrisburg, PA
Pasadena, CA
San Francisco, CA
San Jose, CA

DEPARTMENTS

EarthLink
SK EarthLink

THE STATS

Employer Type: Public Company
Stock Symbol: ELNK
Stock Exchange: NASDAQ
President, CEO and Director: Charles G. Betty
2004 Employees: 2,067
2004 Revenue ($mil.): $1,382.2

KEY COMPETITORS

America Online
AT&T
Microsoft

EMPLOYMENT CONTACT

www.earthlink.net/about/careers

THE SCOOP

The customer is always right

When EarthLink entered onto the ISP scene in 1994, AOL dominated the market. Today, although AOL still dwarfs the Atlanta-based Internet service provider, boasting 29 million subscribers compared to its own 5 million, EarthLink has nonetheless made a name for itself. The company has earned a reputation for stellar customer service, which it achieves through short wait times, a tough-on-spam policy, easy-to-use customizable features and high-quality connectivity. According to the J.D. Power and Associates 2004 Internet Service Provider Residential Customer Satisfaction Survey, EarthLink ranks the highest in customer satisfaction among high-speed and dial-up ISPs.

Connectivity and beyond

EarthLink's primary business is connectivity, whether it be dial-up, high-speed broadband or wireless. The ISP also offers web hosting for businesses and software and tools to block spyware and viruses, eliminate spam and pop-ups, implement parent controls and improve Internet speed. EarthLink recently introduced Voice-over-IP (VoIP) telephone services, which allow users to make local and long distance calls using their broadband connection. Just like a regular telephone, EarthLink's unlimited voice options include features such as call waiting, call forwarding, caller ID block and voicemail. Users can also add a secondary virtual phone number in any area code, transforming a long distance call from friends or family into a local one.

Acquiring subscribers

Over the years, EarthLink has grown its subscriber base through a series of strategic acquisitions, In February 2000, EarthLink boosted its users from around 2 million to 3.5 million through its merger with fellow ISP Mindspring. The move was a savvy one, as it enabled both parties to join forces against fierce competition from newcomers like NetZero, which attracted subscribers by providing free Internet access, while generating revenue via targeted advertising. More recently, in April 2005, EarthLink added to its numbers through the acquisition of Hawk Communications' subscriber base. EarthLink even has a section of its web site devoted to potential acquisition targets. ISPs can fill out an online form to initiate a conversation with EarthLink about the possibility of a buyout.

Catching up

Twenty-something EarthLink founder Sky Dayton claims to be a "Generation X techie who absolutely defies that stereotype." Whatever that means. All we know is that, at the ripe old age of 33, Dayton is onto his next project—high end wireless service. Dayton has become CEO of a joint venture between EarthLink and SK Telecom, Korea's largest wireless-service provider. The wireless service offerings, expected to launch in early 2006, will include music, games, TV and video clips and will be delivered through Sprint and Verizon Wireless. The idea is to bring the United States up to speed; this kind of technology is commonplace in Asia.

GETTING HIRED

How to apply

Interested individuals can apply for jobs at EarthLink or its new joint venture, SK EarthLink, via the company's web site (see careers@EarthLink). The ISP offers jobs in the areas of customer care, facilities services, finance, human resources, information technology, IT support, product and development, project management, and sales and marketing. Techies out there might be interested to know that *ComputerWorld* ranked EarthLink one of the "100 Best Places to Work for IT professionals" in 2005.

OUR SURVEY SAYS

Moving fast

"We're a very fast-growing company in a very quickly changing industry," explains one employee, "so there's not much room for people who want to coast along." As *Microtimes* put it, "Earthlink is on the bleeding edge of technology." The work environment is "very fast paced" and "demanding," but at the same time, "very energetic and positive." The employee population is "very progressive" and "very diverse." In fact, some often joke that "we have one of every kind of person on the planet." "All in all it's just a very friendly, intelligent, enthusiastic group of people who are committed to doing a great job every day."

"People that produce the results have good prospects for promotion," and insiders note that "management strongly encourages all employees to further their education and their careers." "There is the expectation that everyone will want to go on to bigger and better positions," said one source. The company even sends out e-mails to the staff announcing job openings. "Everyone I know that has left EL has gone on to bigger and better things," said one former employee, "but what's unusual is the fact that so have the people that have stayed there."

Typical work hours are 9 to 6, "but if you want to be on the fast track, then expect to do overtime when needed." "There are the occasional late nights," one source said, "but nothing different from any growing company." As far as dress codes, "Earthlink feels everyone works best when they are most comfortable, so nearly anything goes." "The only time anybody wears a suit is when they absolutely have to for a special meeting or such." Employees enjoy an extensive list of perks: there are "between 25 to 30 company-sponsored events" each year, "including discounted plays, sporting events and a company picnic at Disneyland." There is also on-site computer training, yoga classes and massage therapy every other week. The benefits program was recently upgraded and now includes "better health coverage," paid holidays, vacation and sick time, a stock option plan, plus life and disability insurance. Pay is "competitive for the marketplace," and every employee receives "a year-end bonus based on company performance for that year."

Visit Vault at **www.vault.com** for insider company profiles, expert advice, career message boards, expert resume reviews, the Vault Job Board and more.

VAULT CAREER LIBRARY   91

eBay Inc.

2145 Hamilton Avenue
San Jose, CA 95125
Phone: (408) 376-7400
Fax: (408) 376-7401
www.ebay.com

LOCATION

San Jose, CA (HQ)

THE STATS

Employer Type: Public Company
Stock Symbol: EBAY
Stock Exchange: NASDAQ
Chairman: Pierre M. Omidyar
CEO: Margaret C. (Meg) Whitman
2004 Employees: 8,100
2004 Revenue ($mil.): $3,271.3

KEY COMPETITORS

Amazon.com
uBid
Yahoo!

EMPLOYMENT CONTACT

www.ebaycareers.com

THE SCOOP

An Internet powerhouse

One of the true Internet success stories, eBay has mushroomed into the world's largest online bazaar. The site offers 45,000 categories of merchandise, from collectibles and books to computers and real estate. Despite competition from other cyber-markets offered by the likes of Yahoo! and Amazon.com, the rapidly growing eBay continues to build on its phenomenal success through new services, joint ventures, acquisitions and site launches around the world. With more than 90 million registered users and steady profitability, the San Jose, Calif.-based company has won the hearts of collectors and investors alike.

Pioneering the online auction

Pierre Omidyar founded eBay in 1995, when his then-fiancée was having trouble finding a place to buy vintage Pez dispensers. Started as an online auction service on Labor Day weekend in 1995, Omidyar's brainchild was first known as Auction Web and incorporated in 1996. The company name was changed to eBay in 1997. In September of the following year, the company's IPO made quite a splash; its stock soared from $18 a share to a high of $321 on its first day of trading. Perhaps gross margins of 80 percent encouraged traders—along with the fact that eBay had been profitable since shortly after its inception (and still is). Although eBay's stock price has floated back down to Earth since its all-time high in March 2000, the company has managed to keep generating healthy profits while many of its dot-com counterparts have not. eBay stock has one of the top-ranked valuations of any U.S. company, far exceeding that of technology giants like Microsoft Corp. The company makes money by charging sellers a listing fee and through advertising. It also earns commissions, generally from 1 to 5 percent, on each trade. Buyers use the service for free. eBay keeps costs down by making do without inventory, warehouses, sales force or shipping costs. And it has almost no debt.

Year after year, the online community at eBay has only continued to grow. Peer reviews and rating systems for buyers and sellers—an internal "police" force to minimize fraud in listings and expel offenders—and bulletin boards and chat rooms have all been added to the web site. The company also keeps providing new ways to expedite transactions for members. Buyers can purchase products with auction-style bids or at fixed prices through a feature called Buy-It-Now or at Half.com, which is owned by eBay. In September 2004, eBay scrapped previous plans to shut Half.com

Visit Vault at www.vault.com for insider company profiles, expert advice, career message boards, expert resume reviews, the Vault Job Board and more.

VAULT CAREER LIBRARY

93

down and merge it into its existing operations, after many of Half.com's users voiced their disapproval. Marketplace services include an online payment-processing system through subsidiary PayPal, which allows buyers to pay eBay vendors who can't afford a merchant credit-card account; Preferred Solution Provider programs, which match businesses with the software and the services of qualified companies to help sell products on eBay; and a vast array of buyer and seller tools.

A phenomenal streak

Despite a weak economy, 2001 was another great year for eBay, as revenue rose more than 73 percent to $749 million and profits almost doubled to $90 million from the previous year. For 2002, eBay aimed to generate $1.1 billion in revenue, and was shooting for the $3 billion sales mark by 2005 (which the company actually achieved by 2004). As part of that ambitious goal, the company began focusing more on big-ticket items, such as real estate and automobiles, and raised its fees on some listings, such as real estate. The strategies seem to be paying off in spades: eBay members bought and sold $14.87 billion in yearly gross merchandise sales in 2002.

Whitman in charge

Meg Whitman joined eBay as CEO in 1998, when the company's top-selling product was Beanie Babies. Since then, she has helped strengthen eBay's brand recognition and has earned a reputation as one of the best CEOs in the U.S. Among the many to recognize Whitman, *Fortune* magazine ranked her the third most powerful woman in business in 2002; *Worth* magazine ranked her No. 1 on its 2002 list of best CEOs; and *BusinessWeek* magazine has listed her among the 25 most powerful business managers each year since 2000. In September 2003, CBS *MarketWatch* named Whitman the recipient of its first CEO of the Year Award.

Her success stems not just from her years of experience in corporate America (at Hasbro, FDT, Stride Rite and Disney), but also from her hands-on approach. Every day, she and other executives review excerpts from eBay's discussion boards. When they spot a trend among users, they respond, sometimes by creating a new category on the web site, or by making changes to existing ones. Whitman also publicizes her e-mail address to the eBay user community, and as she remarked in a 2003 *BusinessWeek* interview, she makes a point of reading all her own e-mail messages, which can run to as many as 500 a day. Her goal now is to push eBay beyond its roots as an online auction house into an even bigger, all-purpose shopping site and to retain the company's focus on financials. As Whitman declared at an analyst conference in

2001, "This is a whole new way of doing business. We're creating something that didn't exist before." Because eBay has proven such a wildly successful startup, some experts would concur with Whitman that the company presents nothing short of a self-regulating economy.

Branching out

In April 1999, eBay acquired an offline counterpart, the San Francisco auction house Butterfield & Butterfield, which was founded in 1865. eBay made the $260 million purchase in order to attract a new body of users trading high-end items like fine arts, antiques and expensive collectibles online. The company continued to diversify in June 2000, when it moved into the fixed-price trading marketplace by buying Internet retailer Half.com. And in January 2002, eBay signed an alliance with the 258-year-old auction house Sotheby's to integrate Sothebys.com and the eBay Premier site. The deal allows eBay users to take part in many of Sotheby's traditional auctions in New York and London.

But in August 2002, eBay sold Butterfields, the new name of Butterfield & Butterfield, to the London-based Bonhams Auctioneers. While the move was consistent with eBay's desire to move away from an exclusive auctioneering focus, the company was said to have sold its venerable acquisition for far less than it paid in 1999. Butterfields' offline business matters turned out to be more than eBay could reasonably handle, and the company had to concede its relative inexperience in more conventional auction spheres. Over the course of the three-year union, eBay saw plummeting profits at the centuries'-old auction house and was finally forced to lay off what some said was over 50 percent of Butterfields' staff. After the sale to Bonhams, which can now claim a North American presence for the first time, Butterfields continues to pay eBay commissions for products sold on its site.

eBay goes upscale

The different terms of the 2002 joint venture with Sotheby's have produced happier results. The auction house's web site, Sothebys.com, was integrated into eBay's marketplace, where users can avail themselves of upscale auction items from Sotheby's dealers and regional auction houses worldwide, in addition to former high-end eBay dealers. Because eBay isn't saddled with managing unwieldy offline business functions for the auction house, the transition has been a much smoother one. The partnership also marked a definite improvement over Sotheby's past online alliance with Amazon.com, which failed to help either company and ended in

Visit Vault at **www.vault.com** for insider company profiles, expert advice, career message boards, expert resume reviews, the Vault Job Board and more.

VAULT CAREER LIBRARY   95

October 2000, after Amazon reported expenditures of $45 million. By combining Sotheby's reputation with eBay's customer traffic, management hopes to create a niche market of fine art, antiques and collectibles that will increase revenue and profits for each company.

In 2003, eBay acquired FairMarket, Inc., a top provider of online auction and promotional software. The deal was first announced in June 2003, and shareholders at FairMarket approved the sale of the company's business and technology assets for $4.5 million in cash. The deal will not have any substantial effect on 2003 earnings, but the acquisition of the company, which was renamed Dynabazaar, seems like the logical next step, after the year-long commercial relationship between eBay and FairMarket, in the creation of third-party promotions and loyalty programs.

Dominating the international market

Not only does eBay dominate the U.S. online auction market, it reigns supreme overseas with operations in 18 countries. In Europe, eBay is the dominant player in several countries, thanks to its 1999 acquisition of German competitor Alando and its purchase of France's iBazar in 2001. Yahoo!'s exit from many European countries in 2002 further cemented eBay's leading position. eBay strengthened its European stronghold by establishing PayPal's European headquarters and a customer service center in Dublin. The plan created some 800 new jobs. In October 2002, the company announced that PayPal transactions could be completed in Euros or Pounds Sterling in addition to U.S. dollars.

eBay did decide to exit the Japanese market, where Yahoo! is the leading online auction site. However, the company still has high hopes for success in the Asian market. In July 2003, eBay completed its investment in EachNet, the leading e-commerce company in China, by acquiring all the remaining outstanding common stock of the Delaware-based EachNet Inc. The two companies first formed a strategic relationship in March 2002, when eBay obtained a 33 percent interest in EachNet. The remaining 67 percent of EachNet stock was acquired by eBay for $150 million cash in a deal that was first disclosed in June 2003.

A little egg on the face

But the company was forced to adjust its second-quarter earnings for 2003 after a court ruling that awarded nearly $30 million to a Virginia inventor. In 2001, Thomas G. Woolston, founder of the company MercExchange, had sued eBay for knowingly violating his patents on a system to sell fixed-price items on the Internet that drew on an automated payment system. A jury found in favor of Woolston in May 2001, ordering eBay to pay damages to MercExchange to the tune of $35 million. In August 2003, a U.S. district court judge revised the amount of damages to $29.5 million and stopped short of prohibiting eBay from using the same technology that Woolston used to hawk fixed-price goods. But eBay's challenge to the legitimacy of the patents, which pertain to the Buy-It-Now option on the company's auction site, was denied. Both parties were less than satisfied with the ruling; eBay hopes to reverse the judgment or further reduce the amount of damages, while MercExhange wants more money and a permanent ban on eBay's selling fixed-price items. In October 2004, eBay asked for a new trial, claiming the federal jury was instructed improperly regarding the date Woolston said he came up with the idea. Litigation is still pending as of the 2005.

Facing criticism

eBay has, of course, had its share of problems. Many users have complained of sellers using multiple e-mails to bid up their items, sellers who never deliver or buyers who fail to follow through. eBay was also criticized for allowing the sale of firearms, which it has since banned. In 2003, the company canceled an auction to resell a music download that had been bought through Apple Computer's iTunes Music Store. Stating that the sale would violate its listings policies, eBay seemed to be taking a decisive stance—for now, at least—against the resale of music purchased in digital form.

Besides the patent-infringement lawsuits filed by Woolston, eBay also faced a breach of contract claim in 2003 from Stamps.com, which offers online postage services. The suit, which was filed against both eBay and PayPal (which is owned by eBay), charged that PayPal did not do enough to promote Stamps.com technology for PayPal users. The service was supposed to be made available to PayPal users by the holiday season of 2002, allowing those users to purchase and print postage online, but Stamps.com said the company failed to live up to its contractual agreement. An undisclosed settlement was reached in July 2004.

Standing tall in 2003

After an outstanding fourth quarter of 2003, posting a $648 million net revenue, the company reported a $2.17 billion total revenue for the full year (a whopping 78 percent increase over the previous year). Offerings that year included a new suite of shipping tools, launched in conjunction with UPS throughout the eBay marketplace

Visit Vault at **www.vault.com** for insider company profiles, expert advice, career message boards, expert resume reviews, the Vault Job Board and more.

VAULT CAREER LIBRARY   **97**

for shoppers' greater convenience; QuikDrop franchises in 38 states that makes it easier for eBay sellers to prepare and list their items; and the introduction of the PayPal Buyer Protection program, which permits verified Pay Pal sellers with a proven history on eBay to offer buyer protection insurance of up to $500 with no service fee, part of stepped-up efforts by eBay to protect Internet privacy and combat fraud, which only accounts for one-tenth of one percent of all eBay transactions but disproportionately affects high-ticket items like automobiles and computers. In September 2003, eBay even joined forces with other e-commerce giants like Amazon and Microsoft to curb identity theft. The newly formed Coalition on Online Identity Theft revealed plans for a public education campaign and close cooperation with law enforcement officials in their efforts to fight criminals who dupe their victims into disclosing credit card information and other sensitive matters online.

World wide domination

eBay continued its European expansion in 2004, where it now operates local web sites in 11 different countries, with the purchase of German online classifieds provider Mobile.de. The company expects Europe to eventually generate as much revenue as its North American operations. eBay also continued to penetrate the growing Asian market with the acquisition of Indian online marketplace Bazee Pvt, in August 2004. By the middle of 2005, eBay was garnering nearly half of its revenue from outside the U.S., though all hasn't been quiet on the home front. In August 2004, the company acquired a 25 percent interest in craigslist, an Internet forum and classified ad community.

Investor concerns

For the full 2004, eBay pulled in a profit of $829.5 million, up 68 percent from the year prior, but still just under analysts' forecasts. Sales rose 51 percent to $3.27 billion. A slowdown in international dealings led to a material decline in revenue in the fourth quarter, subsequently causing a slip on the stock market. Chief financial officer Rajiy Dutta said the company would expand PayPal, which kicked in $200.2 million in revenue in the fourth quarter of 2004, into new markets in 2005.

The fiscal year 2005 started off on shaky ground. eBay lowered its outlook for revenue growth, though still predicting a 31 percent year-over-year increase. Combine that with a rise in seller fees, increased competition from rivals like Overstock.com and uBid, and rumors that CEO Whitman was being courted for the chief job at Walt Disney, and you no doubt raise suspicion among investors. Stock plummeted 35 percent in the first quarter. Investors were also skeptical of eBay's expansion plans abroad, such as its decision to not charge fees in China, one of the world's largest markets (the company wanted to first build interest).

Shopping for an acquisition

If analysts were unimpressed, eBay's core buyers and sellers did not take notice. The company pulled in quarterly sales of $1 billion for the first time in March 2005, beating Wall Street expectations, while the number of registered users increased 40 percent to 147.1 million. CEO Whitman sees "tremendous" growth in China, India and Korea in the future, and by the end of 2005, eBay plans to offer its PayPal service in China.

To boost its bottom line, eBay picked up Shopping.com Ltd., an online shopping-comparison site, in June 2005 for $620 million. The plan is to integrate eBay listings with those on Shopping.com so sellers can reach a wider pool of buyers. Also that month, eBay opened a marketplace for manufacturers and wholesale merchants to trade with eBay sellers through a program called "Reseller Marketplace." Fueled by growth in its U.S. market, eBay posted a 53 percent increase in second-quarter profit in July 2005, momentarily quelling investor concerns. CFO Dutta attributed the gain to a host of new features, revamped marketing and enhanced communication with sellers.

Et tu Yahoo!?

Rival Yahoo! rained on the firm's revival parade in August 2005 with its $1 billion purchase of Alibaba.com Corp., a rival in the Chinese online auction market. China is quickly becoming the world's most Internet savvy population—by 2009, experts expect more Chinese citizens to be online than any other country in the world, including the United States. eBay's Chinese operations have yet to turn a profit, and more competition would likely make things worse. In the meantime, eBay has joined with government officials in Shanghai to open a "job garden," or business center for would-be online vendors. eBay's EachNet business, based in Shanghai, has also increased advertising via television commercials. But Alibaba's TaoBao service has proven to be more popular, increasing its transaction volume on average 64 percent for each month of 2004. eBay plans to invest $100 million in China in 2005—cash straight from its bottom line—to prevent losing out in a major Asian market to Yahoo! a second time. (eBay pulled out of Japan in 2002 after falling behind to Yahoo! Japan.)

Visit Vault at **www.vault.com** for insider company profiles, expert advice, career message boards, expert resume reviews, the Vault Job Board and more.

VAULT CAREER LIBRARY

99

The height of ambition

To offset the competition, eBay plans to build its U.S. businesses, expand its PayPal services, move aggressively into China and India, and increase its presence in Europe and Asia. Dutta says U.S. revenue remains the largest contributor to growth in dollar terms, and has "lots of running room." Dutta also believes that, in the future, offline commerce will begin to make the jump to online transactions, and that online sales could even end up surpassing catalog sales. The company is also working to close the gap "between safety and trust," making the Internet buying and selling business more attractive to users turned off by identity theft and phishing scams.

Investors have no doubt that eBay can grow its businesses; it remains to be seen whether the firm will continue its market dominance on a global scale. Towards this end, eBay recently increased its international scope with the September 2005 purchase of Skype Technologies, an Internet phone company based in Luxembourg, for $2.6 billion in cash and stock. The deal brings Skype's 54 million users in 225 countries and territories to the eBay fold, along with some impressive statistics—in North America alone, Skype has more users and serves more voice minutes than any other Internet voice communications provider.

GETTING HIRED

Application basics

eBay lists job opportunities on its web site at www.ebaycareers.com. Interested applicants can create an online job profile and search for current openings in North America or abroad (Austria, Belgium, China, France, Germany, Italy, the Netherlands, Spain, Switzerland and the U.K.). eBay also accepts unsolicited resumes for U.S. positions sent via an online form (which requires a log-in name and password). Jobs are available for new college graduates and MBAs in a range of fields, such as marketing, finance, software development, IT and quality assurance. For undergraduate and graduate students trying to get a foot in the door, the company's University Community Internship Program provides valuable work experience and the possibility of full-time employment with eBay after graduation. A recruiting calendar can be found online with more detailed information about dates and schools visited by eBay. Students can attend events on campus or submit a resume through the web site.

Use the Internet's
MOST TARGETED
job search tools.

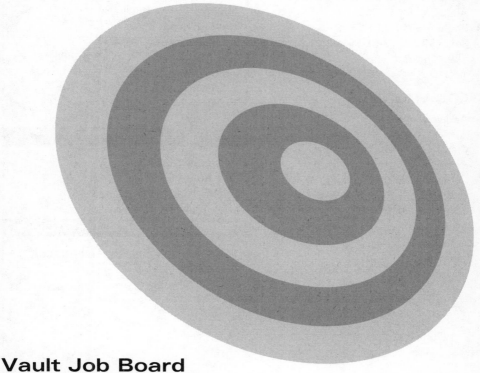

Vault Job Board

Target your search by industry, function and experience level, and find the job openings that you want.

VaultMatch Resume Database

Vault takes match-making to the next level: post your resume and customize your search by industry, function, experience and more. We'll match job listings with your interests and criteria and e-mail them directly to your inbox.

Entrust, Inc.

1 Hanover Park
16633 Dallas Parkway, Suite 800
Addison, TX 75001
Phone: (972) 713-5800
Fax: (972) 713-5805
www.entrust.com

LOCATIONS

Addison, TX (HQ)
Apex, CA • McLean, VA • Santa
Clara, CA • Admiralty, Hong Kong •
Beijing • Montréal • Munich •
Ottawa • Paris • Reading, UK •
Stockholm • Sydney • Tokyo •
Toronto • Vancouver

THE STATS

Employer Type: Public Company
Stock Symbol: ENTU
Stock Exchange: NASDAQ
Chairman & CEO: F. William (Bill)
Conner
2004 Employees: 491
2004 Revenue ($mil.): $91.0

KEY COMPETITORS

Computer Associates
RSA Security
Tumbleweed Communications

EMPLOYMENT CONTACT

www.entrust.com/careers/index.htm

THE SCOOP

Trusted name

Entrust's software and services provide privacy for electronic communications and transactions across corporate networks and the Internet. They focus on issues such as identification, verification, privacy and security primarily through a mix of smart cards, passwords and biometric devices. The company also offers services such as consulting, deployment and managed security.

Security firsts

Entrust built and sold its first commercially available public-key infrastructure (PKI) in 1994, making it possible for businesses to manage keys and certificates for encryption and digital signatures. Two years later, the firm released the industry's first client software to maximize the benefits of PKI and make security easier for users. TruePass, released in 1999, made headlines as the first web-security product to earn FIPS 140-1 validation by both the U.S. and Canadian federal governments.

The acquisition of enCommerce in May 2000 combined the firms' authentication and authorization technologies into a single security infrastructure. Entrust's PKI technology went on to serve as the foundation for the prototype of the U.S. Federal Bridge Certification Authority, which provides secure communications for intergovernmental and cross-governmental secure communications. Entrust GateAccess was also the first web portal security product to cover millions of users in live deployment.

Reorganization

F. William Conner, a former president at Nortel Networks eBusiness Solutions, joined as president and CEO in April 2001. Entrust then announced it would cut 30 percent of its workforce that June, as part of a reorganization towards functional lines, rather than independent business units. In May 2003, the company reorganized its staff, closed some office space and sliced an undisclosed number of jobs again in an effort to break even, as revenue slipped and loss margins widened.

International recognition

In mid-2004, Entrust acquired AmikaNow! Corporation's advanced content scanning, analysis and compliance technology, thus boosting its Secure Messaging

Visit Vault at **www.vault.com** for insider company profiles, expert advice, career message boards, expert resume reviews, the Vault Job Board and more.

V/\ULT CAREER LIBRARY   **103**

and Data Solutions unit. By the end of the year, the company had formed a joint venture with Hong Kong-based Asia Digital Media to deliver secure technology solutions for HDTV satellite broadcasting, high-speed Internet, and online transaction services to the Chinese market.

At the start of 2005, it seemed the firm's financial fortunes were on the rise: Entrust reported a net income of $2.6 million in the quarter ended that January, and revenue of $27.1 million, compared with $23.7 million the year prior. At the end of the second quarter reported July 2005, revenue came in at $24.8 million, a 27 percent increase over the year prior, while transactions increased 97 percent over the second quarter of 2004, and 20 percent over the first quarter of 2005. New business included contracts with the U.S. Department of State for digital signature technology and the Spanish government for digital certificate technology.

GETTING HIRED

Trust-worthy career

Entrust posts job offerings on its career web site, www.entrust.com/careers/index.htm. Applicants can also e-mail the firm's HR department at hrinternational@entrust.com for more information.

E*TRADE FINANCIAL Corp.

135 E. 57th Street
New York, NY 10022
Phone: (646) 521-4300
Fax: (888) 276-9771
www.etrade.com

LOCATIONS

New York, NY (HQ)
Alhambra, CA • Alpharetta, GA •
Beverly Hills, CA • Boston, MA •
Chicago, IL • Costa Mesa, CA •
Dallas, TX • Denver, CO • Orlando,
FL • Palo Alto, CA • San Diego, CA •
San Francisco, CA • Scottsdale, AZ •
Washington, DC

Operations in:
France • Hong Kong • Italy •
Sweden • Switzerland • Taiwan •
United Kingdom • United Arab
Emirates

THE STATS

Employer Type: Public Company
Stock Symbol: ET
Stock Exchange: NYSE
Chairman: George A. Hayter
CEO: Mitchell H. (Mitch) Caplan
2004 Employees: 3,300
2004 Revenue ($mil.): $2,215.8

KEY COMPETITORS

Ameritrade
Charles Schwab
TD Waterhouse

EMPLOYMENT CONTACT

https://us.etrade.com/e/t/home/about
 us?gxml=rjs_listing.html

THE SCOOP

Making money the new-fashioned way

Leading a modern breed of cyber-brokers, E*TRADE FINANCIAL can make a stock market player out of anyone with a computer. The New York-based brokerage firm offers research and lets customers (3.5 million and counting) trade stock electronically via the Internet and touch-tone telephones. The firm also provides cash-and-portfolio management services. For experienced traders, E*TRADE offers up its Professional Trading division, a direct access brokerage firm. But the firm offers more than just trading. Since 2000, E*TRADE has grown into an investment-lending and banking firm.

Virtual trading along the way

E*TRADE was founded by physicist William Porter in 1991 as a subsidiary of his company TradePlus. The new firm took off the next year, when it debuted as CompuServe's first online securities trading service. E*TRADE went public in 1996, and formed E*TRADE Online Ventures, a subsidiary, for exploring the company's growth potential. Hoping to edge out competitors, the firm cut its commissions by 25 percent, lowering transaction fees considerably. The last cuts occured in 2005. Though it suffered slight losses, revenue more than doubled to nearly $52 million. The following year, the company launched a web-based trading service for America Online users.

Some partnerships

Strategic partnerships have been critical to E*TRADE's success over the years. It has allied with various companies for content, promotional programs, distribution and technology. In 2001, E*TRADE became an early adopter of Linux. The company completed a conversion to ADP's back office in 2004. In 2005, E*TRADE began offering SecurID tokens with RSA.

Foreign operations

E*TRADE has also expanded beyond U.S. borders. It launched a service in Canada in February 1997. E*TRADE Australia was established in April 1998. It also set up a joint venture in Japan with Softbank Corp., now the company's largest stockholder. Next came development of the first online-only brokerage in the U.K. In December

2001, the company acquired nearly 5,000 accounts in Hong Kong from 2Cube, a joint venture between J.P. Morgan Chase and Pacific Century Cyberworks. E*TRADE currently has 14 branded web sites worldwide.

Buying spree

Besides partnerships and aggressive international expansion, E*TRADE has a history of making acquisitions. In June 2000, E*TRADE bought its Canadian license holder, Versus Technologies Inc., for $174 million in stock, in a move to expand its brokerage services and gain access to Versus' stock trading system. The acquisition helped expand E*TRADE's range, adding several thousand Canadian online investors to E*TRADE's then 2 million-plus account base and giving the company access to Canadian financial institutions.

More than just trading

In 2000, E*TRADE began an aggressive strategy to become a full-service online financial services firm. It bought Telebanc Financial in January of that year to add to E*TRADE Bank. In June, it announced plans for a series of street-level retail branches. Also that year, E*TRADE sold its investment bank to Wit Capital. In October 2001, the company bought Dempsey & Co., a privately held specialist and market-making firm, for $174 million. Later that month, the company's bank operation acquired more than 33,000 accounts, valued at $1.5 billion, from Chase Manhattan Bank. E*TRADE Bank subsequently launched home equity-based lines of credit and installment loans. Market-making services broadened in February 2002, when E*TRADE established such a service in the U.K. and announced it would look to further expand its market-making operations in Europe.

Strong results

In the summer of 2002, the company's acquisitions continued, as E*TRADE bought Tradescape, an on-site active trading platform, in June for $100 million. In July, E*TRADE reported second quarter financial results that topped analysts' estimates. The company posted earnings for the quarter of $32.8 million, a strong step up from the $10.2 million loss reported in the previous year's second quarter. Revenue rose to $316 million from $308 million. Though sales tied to the company's brokerage business slipped a bit to $215 million from 2001's $229 million tally, the banking division more than made up for that shortfall, as revenue for that division grew to $100 million from just under $79 million.

Visit Vault at www.vault.com for insider company profiles, expert advice, career message boards, expert resume reviews, the Vault Job Board and more.

VAULT CAREER LIBRARY   107

All is not lost

At the start of 2003, Mitchell Caplan signed on as E*TRADE's CEO. Prior to the promotion, Caplan had been both president and COO at the firm. The following year also started off with some big, though disappointing, news: E*TRADE and Toronto-Dominion Bank formally ended talks in January 2004 to merge TD Waterhouse with E*TRADE in a multibillion dollar deal that would have made the combined company the nation's top online brokerage firm. E*TRADE tried wooing Ameritrade Holding Corp, another rival, in May 2005 with a $1.5 billion bid, but came up empty handed yet again, after Ameritrade's board declared the company was not for sale. To add insult to injury, TD Waterhouse and Ameritrade agreed to merge the following month.

E*TRADE remained strong despite the announcement, and maintained it would continue to actively look towards new acquisitions—such as a $700 million deal for rival Harrisdirect from BMO Financial Group of Canada in August 2005, which added 430,000 new active high-value customer accounts, boosting E*TRADE's total account number past 4 million. The same month, E*TRADE also announced plans to buy Kobren Insight Management, an investment adviser managing roughly $1 billion for private clients. Also in 2005, E*TRADE acquired Brown Co.

GETTING HIRED

Trading up

Visit the job section of E*TRADE's web site for details on openings. Applicants may send resumes and cover letters to the company via e-mail. There are links to information about E*TRADE's college recruiting schedule, which is updated annually. The firm also runs an internship program at a number of E*TRADE locations nationwide, focusing on customer service, finance, marketing, human resources and trading. Applicants are advised to sign up for an on-campus interview, or send a resume to internships@etrade.com if their college is not on the company's recruiting list.

OUR SURVEY SAYS

The young and the diverse

Sources say E*TRADE has "an interesting mix of Silicon Valley cubes/geeks and conservative financial services people." "Most of our employees are in their 20s or 30s," one employee said. "Everyone is very friendly, and the place has a collegiate feel." E*TRADE encourages the fun by sponsoring frequent company get-togethers. "We had a department water fight the other day, and a barbecue on site," reports one insider. "The culture is really relaxed." Diversity is also key at E*TRADE. "There are no boundaries about race, gender, sexual preference or religion. Your co-workers judge you by what you produce and how nice you are, not by superficial things." Many of the company's managers and "the majority of E*TRADE's executive team" are women, including the CCO and the CGAO. "They are some of the highest paid people in Silicon Valley," revealed one employee.

Open season

As expected, E*TRADE "has no real dress code," though "those who deal with customers and clients dress corporate casual most days." "An unwritten Friday free-for-all is also the norm," said one source. The company is also flexible about work schedules, which usually average 40 hours per week. Starting salaries are "kind of low," but "consistent with scales for the San Francisco Bay Area for the financial services industry." Employees report lots of opportunities for advancement, and say "it's a great start for someone right out of college." On the down side, the company is experiencing the inevitable "growing pains" associated with rapid expansion. "Sometimes there are glitches with the web site and customers call and are upset, but the system is constantly being upgraded to handle faster and better service." Perks include "liberal stock option grants," discounts on trading commissions, frequent catered working lunches and "lots of free stuff with the company logo."

Visit Vault at www.vault.com for insider company profiles, expert advice, career message boards, expert resume reviews, the Vault Job Board and more.

VAULT CAREER LIBRARY   109

Expedia, Inc.

3150 139th Avenue Southeast
Bellevue, WA 98005
Phone: (425) 564-7200
Fax: (425) 564-7240
www.expedia.com

LOCATIONS

Bellevue, WA (HQ)
22 additional locations worldwide.

DEPARTMENTS

Corporate Travel
eLong
Expedia Asia Pacific
Expedia Europe
Leisure Travel
Partner Services

THE STATS

Employer Type: Public Company
Stock Exchange: NASDAQ
Stock Symbol: EXPE
CEO and Director: Dara Khosrowshahi
2004 Employees: 3,982
2004 Revenue ($mil.): $496.5*
*IAC Travel Revenue. Prior to July 2005,
Expedia was a subsidiary of IAC.

KEY COMPETITORS

Orbitz
Travelocity
Priceline

EMPLOYMENT CONTACT

www.expediainc.com/careers

THE SCOOP

All by myself

Expedia, Inc. sprouted new wings when former parent company, InterActive Corp (IAC) decided to spin off Expedia.com and its related travel services (Hotels.com, Hotwire, TripAdvisor, Expedia Corporate Travel and Classic Vacations) in July 2005. As a standalone company, Expedia is the largest online travel agency in the world.

The company got its start back in 1995 as part of Microsoft. The travel unit was spun off just a year later and in 1999, it went public. In 2001, InterActive Corp (then USA Networks) acquired a controlling stake in the travel company, completing the acquisition in 2002. Though the two companies—IAC and Expedia—are now separate entities, they share a common chairman, Barry Diller, and Expedia's CEO, Dara Khosrowshahi, is IAC's former CFO.

The one, the many

Expedia breaks its business up into six main divisions: North America Leisure Travel Group, Partner Services Group, Expedia CorporateTravel, Expedia EMEA and Expedia Asia Pacific. The company's leisure travel group is focused on—you guessed it—leisure travel and includes Expedia.com, Expedia.ca (Canada), Hotels.com, Hotels.ca, TripAdvisor, Hotwire and Classic Vacations. Expedia Corporate Travel caters to small and midsized businesses and delivers centralized booking tools, support for negotiated airfares and consolidated reporting. Partner Services Group manages the company's relationships with various airline, hotel and car rental partners. Expedia EMEA handles Expedia-branded web sites in France, Germany, Italy, the Netherlands and the UK, as well as Anyway.com, a discount travel seller in France, and Voyages-SNCF.fr in partnership with France's railway company, SNCF. Expedia Asia Pacific is a growing unit responsible for managing the company's activities in the Asia Pacific region. In association with Expedia's expansion into Asia, the company has a majority stake in eLong, which provides online travel services in China.

Visit Vault at **www.vault.com** for insider company profiles, expert advice, career message boards, expert resume reviews, the Vault Job Board and more.

VAULT CAREER LIBRARY   111

GETTING HIRED

The search

Individuals interested in working for Expedia can choose to use "Global Job Search" or go directly to a specific company's career site. The global job search engine allows prospective hires to hunt down positions by business, location and category, and to apply for them online.

Friendster, Inc.

1380 Villa Street
Mountain View, CA 94041
Phone: (650) 618-2638
Fax: (650) 618-2527
www.friendster.com

LOCATION

Mountain View, CA (HQ)

DEPARTMENTS

Engineering/Web Development
Finance
Human Resources
Marketing
Operations
Product Development
Sales

THE STATS

Employer Type: Private Company
Chairman: Jonathan Abrams
CEO: Taek Kwon
2004 Employees: 24

KEY COMPETITORS

craigslist
Intermix Media
Spring Street

EMPLOYMENT CONTACT

www.friendster.com/jobs/index.php
E-mail: jobs@friendster.com

Visit Vault at **www.vault.com** for insider company profiles, expert advice,
career message boards, expert resume reviews, the Vault Job Board and more.

VAULT CAREER LIBRARY   113

THE SCOOP

Friends in high places

Friendster takes the concept of social networking to new extremes via the tag line, "making the world a smaller place, one friend at a time." The company is backed by Kleiner Perkins, Caufield & Byers, Benchmark Capital, Battery Ventures, and a number of Internet heavyweights including former Yahoo! CEO Tim Koogle, former PayPal CEO Peter Thiel and former Amazon.com VP Ram Shriram. Friendster was named as one of *Time* magazine's Coolest Inventions of 2003, and has since been featured in a range of media publications, including CNN, *The Wall Street Journal*, *Rolling Stone*, *Entertainment Weekly*, and *Wired*, and today boasts over 20 million members.

Second time's the charm

Entrepreneur Jonathan Abrams, a former founder and CEO of HotLinks, founded Friendster in March 2003 primarily as a dating site. Abrams had prior experience in the realm of Internet connections through a previous failed venture, SixDegrees.com, released in 1997 to little applause, if only because the World Wide Web had not yet become an international phenomenon. Abrams struck gold with the new business; within six months of going live, Friendster had registered over 290,000 members—a number that was rising at a rate of 20 percent per week by the end of 2003. Google reportedly attempted to buy Friendster for $30 million that December, but Abrams refused, instead turning to a slew of investors for financing to the tune of $13 million. Friendster membership eclipsed 3 million members at the start of 2004, and swelled to 13 million by the end of that year.

Sass-y opportunities

Scott Sassa, a former NBC executive, was brought onboard in June 2004 to further raise revenue. Sassa noted "big opportunity" in using social networks for advertising purposes—specifically, having users, in this case, trusted "friendsters," recommend products to other users. *The Wall Street Journal* called Sassa's hiring "the latest move by Friendster to transform itself from a quirky Internet start-up to a profitable online business." In an effort to entice users to spend more time on the site (thus appeasing advertisers who spent big bucks for strategic ad placements), Sassa experimented with horoscopes and news headlines—both ideas that failed to generate the desired response. Sassa did, however, find some luck with advertisements for NBC's *The*

Apprentice and Dreamworks SKG's *Anchorman* by creating profiles of the candidates and characters, respectively, to promote both projects and to reach out to potential viewers via the Internet.

Friendly competition

Despite the innovations, numbers plagued the friendly firm. Though Friendster boasted 16 million users to rival MySpace's 7.6 million in December 2004, more than five times as many people visited the latter over Friendster, and spent a whopping 78 minutes tooling around on MySpace per visit, as opposed to Friendster's 17-minute average. In addition, MySpace logged more than 2 billion page views the same month, while Friendster recorded a mere 152 million. MySpace eclipsed Friendster in the 18 to 29 demographic for membership by the start of 2005, prompting the departure of a number of senior executives. Analysts claimed the former networking powerhouse "missed a big opportunity" in neglecting to add new features, while industry insiders wondered if social networking would ever turn a profit. Friendster shot back that, because of the influx of membership, their concern was with working on infrastructure to make sure service was stable for users, instead of rolling out new features. Abrams, meanwhile, insisted big things were in store for his brainchild while the company reorganized.

Networking in action

Sassa eventually resigned his post in May 2005, after admitting he "wasn't the right person to go forward" and that the company needed "someone more versed in technology." Taek Kwon, a former executive vice president of IAC/InterActiveCorp's Citysearch unit, was named the new CEO in June, becoming the fourth man to take the helm in just over two years. New features, including a blog function powered by TypePad and a "classifieds" section in conjunction with Pusit.com, a Manila-based online classifieds community company, seem to be garnering interest at the site. The company is also attempting to foster growth through a new "SuperFriendster" program that allows users to add links to Friendster on web pages, blogs, newsletters and e-mails to promote the site. It remains to be seen, though, whether Friendster will maintain popularity, or buckle under the power of the social networking force it created.

Visit Vault at **www.vault.com** for insider company profiles, expert advice, career message boards, expert resume reviews, the Vault Job Board and more.

VAULT CAREER LIBRARY   115

GETTING HIRED

Calling all jobsters

Friendster lists job openings on its career site, www.friendster.com/jobs/index.php. As of January 2006, the company does not have any positions available.

Globix Corporation

139 Centre Street
New York, NY 10013
Phone: (212) 334-8500
Fax: (212) 965-6828
www.globix.com

LOCATIONS

New York, NY (HQ)
Atlanta, GA
Fairfield, NJ
Santa Clara, CA
London

THE STATS

Employer Type: Public Company
Stock Symbol: GEX
Stock Exchange: AMEX
Chairman: Ted S. Lodge
President & CEO: Peter K. Stevenson
2004 Revenue ($mil.): $61.2

KEY COMPETITORS

Level 3 Communications
MCI

EMPLOYMENT CONTACT

www.globix.com/about_careers.html

Visit Vault at **www.vault.com** for insider company profiles, expert advice,
career message boards, expert resume reviews, the Vault Job Board and more.

VAULT CAREER LIBRARY   117

THE SCOOP

One-stop shopping for businesses

You want to get your business on the Internet, but you're still befuddled by the blinking clock on your VCR. Where do you go? If you run a medium- to large-size corporation, you might turn to Globix Corporation, the one-stop shop for ISP customers. For businesses low on time to shop around for Internet services, Globix provides everything from web hosting, co-location (providing monitoring and space for servers) and streaming audio/video, to 3-D animation, database administration, systems administration, network monitoring, e-commerce services and corporate training classes. Clients include Friendster, digidesign, EC3 Solutions and Fox Kids UK.

Father-son duo going public

Founded by Marc Bell in 1989—when he was just 21—Globix has enjoyed increasing demand since Bell began emphasizing the company's Internet services focus in the mid-1990s. He also brought his father, Robert Bell, on board as EVP and CFO in 1994 (Papa Bell switched his title to EVP of business development in 1999). The company went public in March 1999.

Build me a SuperPOPS

Offering data centers for its clients' outsourced servers, Globix realized that it needed to open a branch close to its California clients, and leased a 60,000-square-foot "campus" in Santa Clara, Calif. in November 1998. The following year, Globix opened an office in London, which will serve as its European headquarters. It also built three "SuperPOPS" in London, San Francisco and New York. (SuperPOPS are buildings especially designed for housing servers, with air conditioning, raised floors, fire suppression systems and power generators.)

Bell's hell

With an $80 million investment from Dallas-based venture capital firm Hicks, Muse, Tate & Furst (November 1999) and $250 million in high-yield debt (February 2000), Globix, which held 289,000 square feet of space in September 2000, seemed poised to make good on a plan to expand its computer space to more than a million square feet by the end of 2001. However, after an executive departure (founder Bell cashed in his shares in July 2001 for a reported $100 million) and a bankruptcy filing (in January 2002), Globix was left with barely 78,000 square feet of space—40 percent of which was leased—not to mention a market value that had plunged to $5.87 million, from nearly $1 billion in 1999.

Rebuilding the brand

The company emerged from Chapter 11 during the summer of 2002, with less debt and a new lease on life. Professional services firm Deloitte & Touche LLP took note, and named Globix to its Technology Fast 50 Program for New York, a list of the city's fastest growing technology companies, in 2003. D&T praised Globix for its "tremendous accomplishments during economically challenged times."

In October 2003, Globix agreed to acquire Aptegrity, a managed services provider focused on web-based applications, noting the acquisition was a "key component" of Globix's shift to becoming a full-service managed applications and hosting provider. An even bigger deal followed in July 2004, after Globix agreed to merge with Neon Communications in a transaction worth $10.2 million. More recently, Globix put security measures at the forefront of operations, updating its services and solutions to secure clients from viruses, worms, hackers and other assorted computer threats.

Streaming media leader

Globix has been in charge of webcasting several high-profile events that have helped establish it as a leader in streaming media. Notable webcasts produced by Globix include Bill Gates' keynote address launching Windows 2000, Boxing.com's live webcast of the Tyson/Francis fight, a live webcast of Bon Jovi from the band's recording studio, and A&E's *Live by Request* show with the Eurythmics. Web sites hosted by Globix include music.com, yellowpages.com and lifetimetv.com.

GETTING HIRED

Go global

Check out Globix's career opportunities page at career.pereless.com/index.cfm? CID=75025 for information on applying to the company. Jobs are posted according to operational division. The company also accepts employment inquiries via an

Visit Vault at **www.vault.com** for insider company profiles, expert advice, career message boards, expert resume reviews, the Vault Job Board and more.

V**A**ULT CAREER LIBRARY   **119**

online resume form found at career.pereless.com/index.cfm?fuseaction=jobs.apply &CID=75025&JID=0.

Google

1600 Amphitheatre Parkway
Mountain View, CA 94043
Phone: (650) 623-4000
Fax: (650) 618-1499
www.google.com

LOCATION

Mountain View, CA (HQ)

THE STATS

Employer Type: Public Company
Stock Symbol: GOOG
Stock Exchange: NASDAQ
Chairman and CEO: Eric E. Schmidt
2004 Employees: 3,021
2004 Revenue ($mil.): $3,189.2

KEY COMPETITORS

America Online
Microsoft
Yahoo!

EMPLOYMENT CONTACT

www.google.com/intl/en/jobs/index.
html

Visit Vault at **www.vault.com** for insider company profiles, expert advice,
career message boards, expert resume reviews, the Vault Job Board and more.

VAULT CAREER LIBRARY   121

THE SCOOP

Search engine success

If you've ever conducted an Internet-based search, chances are, you're familiar with Google. One of the world's most popular Internet sites, Google logs 81.9 million worldwide users per month, operates in 35 different languages, and has even spawned the pop culture phenomenon known as "Googling." The company generates revenue primarily through ads targeted by keywords and by selling ads to more than 200,000 affiliated web sites. Founders Sergey Brin and Larry Page took their brainchild public in August 2004; each owns more than 25 percent voting control of the company, which derives its name from the word "googol." Coined by Milton Sirotta, the nephew of American mathematician Edward Kasner, Googol refers to the number represented by the numeral 1 followed by 100 zeros. Brin and Page chose the moniker to represent their ambition to organize the seemingly endless amount of information available on the Web.

The meeting of like minds

When Brin first met Page in 1995, Page was a 24-year-old University of Michigan alumnus visiting the graduate program in computer science at Stanford University. Brin was his designated tour guide. The two found common ground on the then-troubling concept plaguing computer programmers as the Internet began to take flight: how to retrieve relevant information from the millions of sites popping up across the Web. Their first collaboration, started in January 1996, was a search engine called BackRub, named for its ability to analyze "back links" pointing to a given web site. Page, a constant inventor who once built a working printer out of Legos, took up the task of creating a new server. He quickly ran into the age-old problem plaguing most young inventors: lack of capital for resources. Brin and Page soon began digging through Stanford's loading docks, searching for computers they could borrow to set up their network.

Word of the BackRub program soon spread around the Stanford campus. The duo bought a terabyte of disks (maxing out credit cards in the process) and built their own computer housing in Page's dorm room, which later became Google's first unofficial data center. Brin began contacting potential business partners who might be interested in licensing search technology. Among those contacted was David Filo, a friend and co-founder of Yahoo! Filo advised the men to build their own search engine organically, and to get in contact with him when it was "fully developed." On the whole, most CEOs showed little interest in search engines.

If you build it, they will come ...

Brin and Page decided to follow Filo's advice, and try to start a search engine on their own. They put their PhDs on hold, crafted a business plan and began the search for an investor in 1998. Andy Bechtolsheim, one of the founders of Sun Microsystems and a friend of a Stanford faculty member, was immediately sold on Google. Bechtolsheim, recognizing the idea's potential, cut a check for $100,000 made out to Google Inc. At that point, though, there was no Google Inc. Brin and Page spent the next few months scrounging up the capital needed to set up their corporation, knocking on the doors of friends, family and acquaintances, eventually coming up with an initial investment of nearly $1 million.

Thus, in September 1998, Google opened its doors in Menlo Park, Calif. Its first employee, Craig Silverstein, is still with the company today, currently serving as Google's director of technology. Though the Google.com site was still in beta, it began answering up to 10,000 search queries daily. Members of the press started to pick up on the search engine, generating a publicity storm that resulted in *PC Magazine* naming Google as one of its Top 100 Web Sites and Search Engines for 1998, mere months after the company was born.

Creating a "Googleplex"

Google quickly grew out of the Menlo Park space, and moved its office and its eight employees to Palo Alto, Calif., in February 1999. By that point, the service was answering nearly half a million queries on a daily basis. In June 1999, Google secured founding from two leading venture capital firms in Silicon Valley, Sequoia Capital and Kleiner Perkins Caufield & Byers. The two firms lent executives to Google's board, which conducted its meetings around a ping pong table in the Palo Alto office.

Soon, more employees came onboard, many of whom walked away from lofty positions at well-known firms like Microsoft and Netscape to take a chance on the startup. To accommodate Google's growing staff, the company moved again, this time to a location in Mountain View, Calif., dubbed "Googleplex," where its headquarters remain today. Around this time, AOL/Netscape chose Google as its web search service of choice, boosting traffic levels to three million searches daily. The web site removed the "beta" label in September 1999, as notoriety spread to a worldwide level. Virgilio, an Italian portal, and Virgin Net, the U.K.'s online entertainment guide, signed on as clients that fall. The whirlwind year culminated with Google being named to *Time* magazine's Top Ten Best Cybertech list for 1999.

Feeling lucky

In the new millennium, Google began offering a spate of new services to draw users away from competitors, including different language versions; a Google Directory (based on Netscape's Open Directory Project); AdWords, a self-service ad program; a Google toolbar; and capabilities to search via wireless devices. The site even added an "I'm Feeling Lucky" button, which, when clicked instead of the regular "Search" button, brought users directly to the web site Google calculated to be the most closely associated with the search topic.

By June 2000, Google was the world's largest search engine, with a billion-page index. Clients immediately began signing up to use Google search technology on their own web sites, as a keyword-targeted advertising program funneled further revenue into Googleplex. Google and Yahoo! announced a partnership in the same month that solidified Google's existence as a substantial Internet business. China's NetEase portal and NEC's BIGLOBE in Japan both joined the Google family, stretching Google's reach into the Asian market.

Bringing in the big gun

Looking to further expand the business, Google built up a number of partnerships with wireless providers in the first half of 2001 to bring the company's technology to mobile users worldwide. Sprint PCS, Cingular and AT&T Wireless were among those to gain access to Google's index, which, by that point, was home to 1.6 billion web documents. Larry Page stepped down as CEO in August 2001, and was replaced by Dr. Eric Schmidt, a former CEO and chairman at software maker Novell and chief technology officer at Sun Microsystems. Page and Brin handpicked Schmidt for the job, counting on his expertise in the computer industry to help them expand their fledgling business. By the fourth quarter of 2001, three years after its initial founding, Google reached profitability. The company's international dealings grew after new partnerships with Lycos Korea and Universo Online, a Latin American search engine. Sales offices opened in Hamburg, Germany, and Tokyo to handle global business.

Back to the beginning

For its next innovation, Google began where it all started: with the search. Image Search, launched in beta form in the summer of 2001, indexed over 250 million images, while Catalogue Search browsed 1,100 mail-order catalogs previously only available in print. Googlebot, the robotic software that continually refreshes and expands Google's online documents, spawned the Google Search Appliance, a plug-and-play search solution for the corporate world that filtered through a variety of company intranets, networks and organizations. Google's web application programming interfaces allowed software programs to search Google directly, while its Google Compute feature used idle cycles on computers to solve computation-intensive scientific problems. Not surprisingly, Google won top honors at the 2001 Search Engine Watch Awards in Outstanding Search Service, Best Image Search Engine, Best Design, Most Webmaster Friendly Search Engine, and Best Search Feature. In May 2002, America Online called Google "the reigning champ of online search" and formed a partnership with the company to provide search services to some 34 million AOL members. Google News, launched in beta form in September 2002, offered access to 4,500 news sources from around the world, while Froogle, first tested in December 2002, delivered images and prices for specific products to online shoppers.

In 2003, Google acquired Pyra Labs, which became the source of the Blogger, a leading provider of online journals (weblogs). The company ended the year with a $961.9 million revenue on a net profit of $106.5 million, while sales skyrocketed 177 percent. A year later, Google added features such as Local Search, which scours neighborhoods for specific queries, and Gmail, a free e-mail account with an astonishing 1,000 megabytes of memory, at the time 250 times greater and 500 times greater the free storage space offered by Yahoo! and Hotmail, respectively.

Private—keep out!

The Gmail launch was not without its share of controversy, though. Since Google does not slip paid-placement ads into search results, the company decided to try a different approach to advertising—placing ads with relevant content in incoming e-mail messages through Gmail. The Electronic Privacy Information Center declared Gmail "an unprecedented invasion into the sanctity of private communications" and California State Senator Liz Figueroa drafted a bill making it illegal to scan the contents of personal e-mails. Google countered that no actual person would be looking at individual e-mails—computers would do all the scanning, utilizing the same software that scans search pages and online shopping purchases. And, in the

Visit Vault at **www.vault.com** for insider company profiles, expert advice, career message boards, expert resume reviews, the Vault Job Board and more.

VAULT CAREER LIBRARY   125

end, the ease of use with Gmail versus its competitors made it a runaway hit, much like the other Google programs rolled out in recent years.

IPO explosion

Google expanded its efforts in Asia by taking a minority stake in the Chinese-language Internet search company Baidu.com Inc. in June 2004. That summer, Google prepared for its biggest leap of all—going public. The offering was conducted as a Dutch-auction to make shares more widely accessible. Dutch-auctions, which allow all investors to place bids privately, level the playing field between the average Joes looking to pick up a few hundred shares and the mega-million investors buying billions in stock. Brin and Page noted in a statement that it was "important to have a fair process" for the IPO and to "include both large and small investors." At the 11th hour, Google cut its price for the IPO after it appeared demand for the stock was weaker than expected. Of course, the opportunity to get in on such a highly anticipated offering at a lower price resulted in a jump in investor demand. In the first few days of trading, the Google stock—which debuted at $85 a share — had climbed past $100, netting a reported $1.67 billion for the company, less than the proposed $2.7 billion Google suggested it would earn in its initial SEC filing. Critics blamed the stock slip on Google's free-for-all bidding process, which isolated and angered investors by avoiding the typical IPO route of kowtowing to Wall Street big-wigs, thus driving down share price.

No self-promotion here

In October 2004, Google acquired the Keyhole Corporation, a supplier of online satellite maps, to enhance its Google Maps and Google Local services, combining satellite and aerial images with mapping data. Schmidt, Page and Brin all asked for annual salaries of $1 in 2004—a wildly successful year in which, according to many industry analysts, they could have easily demanded seven-figure compensation. The three men had done what few predecessors had accomplished—created a billion-dollar company in under five years out of a dot-com market that claimed the lives of many other start-up companies.

Can't please everyone

Not one to sit on its laurels, Google entered 2005 maintaining its focus on innovation. By the end of the fiscal year reported February 2005, shares peaked at a new 52-week high—$217. Revenue came in at $3.19 billion, up an astounding 118 percent from the year prior, while net income skyrocketed 278 percent to $399.1 million. Meanwhile, the company's CEO and co-founders continue to ask for $1 a year (though all three men are multi-billionaires on paper thanks to stock options). The rise in fortunes wasn't all roses, though. As Google began to try to sign advertising deals directly with Fortune 1000 advertisers, media buyers grew alienated and frustrated. Then, the company announced in July 2005 it would refrain from talking to CNETNews.com for a period of one year after the tech journal wrote an article raising privacy questions about Google's searches. Silicon Valley insiders began using the adjective "arrogant" when describing the former Internet darling, and an August 2005 article in *The New York Times* suggested Google was the heir apparent to the throne of evil once filled by the likes of Bill Gates and Microsoft.

Dominating the Dow

Nonetheless, Google has forged ahead in 2005, picking up Dodgeball.com, a free text-messaging service, and Picasa, a digital photo management company. New on the horizon is a video search engine, which offers searchable video clips through partnerships with CBS News, MTV, Reuters and other news organizations and TV programmers. Web Accelerator, a new downloadable program from Google Labs introduced in May 2005, sends URL requests through company services designed specifically to speed site downloads, improving a computer's overall ability to load web sites. In August 2005, Google released Google Talk, an instant-messaging program for real-team digital communication, and Google Desktop 2, an information-management utility. Meanwhile, Gmail removed the "beta" tag and opened up to the masses.

The markets responded favorably to Google's innovations. In June 2005, the company's shares eclipsed $300 for the first time ever, representing a gain of 260 percent on its initial $85 asking price. However, some analysts view the company as risky since it is, essentially, a "one-trick pony" running off the steam of search-based advertising. Its recent dabbles with e-mail, maps and videos—while taking the Google name to different avenues—all still generate revenue mainly through advertising intrinsically linked with searches. Diversifying for the future is the key to keeping the Google name in the know as rivals like Microsoft and Baidu attempt to revamp their own search engines in an attempt to gain market share.

Visit Vault at **www.vault.com** for insider company profiles, expert advice, career message boards, expert resume reviews, the Vault Job Board and more.

V/\ULT CAREER LIBRARY   **127**

The next big thing

In August 2005, the company announced plans to raise another $4 billion through a secondary stock offering, setting off a firestorm of speculation as to what Google's next big move will be. The company has slowly but steadily been building a cache of unused fiber-optic cable across the country, along with connections from wireless companies between major East Coast cities. Google has also reportedly expressed interested in Feeva, a California startup readying free hotspots in major cities across the U.S., prompting talk that its next foray will be into the world of wireless. Pundits predict Google could go so far as to grant Wi-Fi access to everyone in America through a national broadband network, with offerings like digital-video databases or on-demand television programming.

GETTING HIRED

Hiring overview

Jobs at Google fall into the following categories: engineering, operations and IT; partner services and operations; product development; advertising sales, advertising operations, enterprise sales and support, search services and syndication; corporate communications; marketing; finance; facilities; legal; business and corporate development; business operations; human resources; administrative; and international. Additionally, job seekers with experience in software development, computer science and product management can send a resume and cover letter to greatpeople@google.com. Among the perks for Google employees are daily free gourmet lunches, company picnics, an on-site gym and massage therapist, and on-site doctors and dentists.

HotJobs.com

44 West 18th Street
New York, NY 10011
Phone: (646) 351-5300
Fax: (212) 944-8962
www.hotjobs.com

LOCATIONS

New York, NY (HQ)
Boston, MA
Chicago, IL
Los Angeles, CA
Miami, FL
San Francisco, CA
Toronto

THE STATS

Employer Type: Subsidiary of Yahoo!
Executive VP and General Manager:
Daniel J. Finnegan

KEY COMPETITORS

CareerBuilder.com
Hire.com
Monster.com

EMPLOYMENT CONTACT

www.hotjobs.com

Visit Vault at **www.vault.com** for insider company profiles, expert advice,
career message boards, expert resume reviews, the Vault Job Board and more.

VAULT CAREER LIBRARY   129

THE SCOOP

Hot for Y(ah)oo

A frontrunner in the crowded field of Internet recruiting, HotJobs was founded by Richard Johnson in February 1997. Johnson, who had previously started technical staffing firm OTEC Inc., took HotJobs public in August 1999, raising over $20 million for the fledgling company, and establishing the site as one of the leading online job boards. HotJobs spent the next few years vying with Monster.com and CareerBuilder.com for supremacy in the field. In the summer of 2001, HotJobs agreed to merge with its chief competitor, industry leader Monster.com, but later took a more lucrative offer to be acquired by Internet giant Yahoo! for $436 million.

Yahoo's HotJobs site earns revenue from recruiters, who pay a set fee to have a certain number of jobs featured per month; from banner ads of member companies, who pay for ads and premium placement on the site; and from numerous co-sponsorships. HotJobs also licenses recruiting solutions and hiring management software to employers, recruiters and staffing agencies.

Hot features

HotJobs has several features—free to the job seeker—that aim to alleviate the complications of the job search. For instance, MyHotJobs enables registered members to post a resume, keep track of which HotJobs they've applied for and check how many companies have viewed their resume. Site visitors can also use the HotJobs' Job Agent feature to get a list of new jobs in specific industries e-mailed to them each day. In addition, the HotBlock function allows job seekers to keep their resumes blocked from selected companies. The job search engine's ease-of-use earned the site "Best General Purpose Job Board for Job Seekers" in 2002 and 2003 and the "People's Voice" Webby Award for excellence in web design, creativity, usability and functionality in 2005.

Hot off the press

In July 2005, HotJobs announced a new feature that may make the site even more attractive to job seekers. The company added a new job search engine that searches the Internet, in addition to the company's job database, for job listings. HotJobs reasons that more jobs means more job seekers and thus more qualified candidates for its customers. With an eye on improving job seekers' experience, HotJobs also revamped its image in August 2004, launching a new homepage designed to be more inviting and easier to use.

GETTING HIRED

Hot jobs at HotJobs

HotJobs posts its own job openings on hotjobs.com—and why not? The company reasons that the same user-friendly format that works for customers should work just as well for itself. Prospective employees can access HotJobs openings by clicking on the "Work at HotJobs" link at the bottom of the HotJobs' home page or by going to the HotJobs company profile. The company offers benefits like medical and dental insurance, 401(k) and paid vacation.

Visit Vault at **www.vault.com** for insider company profiles, expert advice, career message boards, expert resume reviews, the Vault Job Board and more.

VAULT CAREER LIBRARY   131

iVillage Inc.

500 7th Avenue, 14th Floor
New York, NY 10018
Phone: (212) 600-6000
Fax: (212) 604-9133
www.ivillage.com

LOCATION

New York, NY (HQ)

THE STATS

Employer Type: Public Company
Stock Symbol: IVIL
Stock Exchange: NASDAQ
Chairman & CEO: Douglas W. (Doug) McCormick
2004 Employees: 216
2004 Revenue ($mil.): $66.9

KEY COMPETITORS

Lifetime
Martha Stewart Living
Oxygen Media

EMPLOYMENT CONTACT

Mail a cover letter and resume to:
Human Resources Department
iVillage Inc.
500 Seventh Avenue, 14th Floor
New York, NY 10018

THE SCOOP

Women Wide Web

The Web isn't just for geeky teenagers anymore, and iVillage has taken notice. One of the first web sites to target women as an audience, iVillage offers up info on topics from careers to child care, plus free e-mail, chat rooms, a book club and online shopping. It even has a pregnancy calendar, which shows a baby's development from conception to birth. It is still one of the most prominent new media companies in New York's Silicon Alley, despite recent troubles in its foray into e-commerce. The company also runs Astrology.com, GardenWeb.com and gURL.com; creates offline content through its *Lamaze Parents* magazine and The Newborn Channel cable network; iVillage Consulting, a web development firm; Promotions.com, a promotional marketing firm; and the Public Affairs Group.

Ample funding

Candice Carpenter, formerly the chief executive of Q2 (the upscale division of the QVC home shopping channel), founded the company in 1995. Her idea was to reach out to the growing numbers of women on the Internet—with a specific focus on baby boomers. Launched with seed money from America Online, the company has been to the venture capital trough four times in its short history. On the last trip, in May 1998, iVillage garnered $32 million—about $12 million more than it had expected. Among its other backers are Intel, Glaxo-Wellcome and the National Bank of Kuwait.

Burn, iBaby, burn

In May 2000 iVillage conceded defeat in one its early attempts to break into the world of e-commerce when it sold off iBaby. The decision to ditch iBaby, which sells everything from strollers to breast pumps, is seen as a significant shift in strategy for iVillage. When the company acquired a $1.35 million majority stake in iBaby in April 1998, it was widely heralded as a groundbreaking strategy in which an online content provider could make customers out of its users. But two years later, iVillage has apparently changed its mind about the tumultuous world of retailing after dealing with the day-to-day annoyances of warehouses and product returns. The about-face in iVillage's strategy comes at a time when the company is ailing from a severely beaten stock value, high turnover among its executives and employees, and growing quarterly losses. In July the company sold iBaby to rival online baby-products retailer BabyGear.com for an undisclosed sum. iVillage has also announced plans to stop maintaining iMaternity.com and PlusBoutique.com, which will now be completely produced by Dan Howard Industries.

Care for a spot of tea?

U.K. cyberwomen rejoice—iVillage has teamed up with food retailer Tesco to produce iVillage U.K. at a time when women increasingly control online spending. Announced in July 2000, the new venture has $70 million for marketing, branding, intellectual property and other resources. The joint venture functions as an independently managed entity.

Chief Candice no more

In mid-2000 notoriously abrasive iVillage CEO Candice Carpenter announced she would step down to assume the role of chairman, while current President Doug McCormick would take over as CEO. Former COO Allison Abraham and former CFO Craig Monaghan had both left iVillage in May, sparking rumors that Carpenter had been too demanding. Carpenter noted that McCormick's appointment to the position of CEO had been part of her plan from the time he joined the board of directors two years before. In July 2000, iVillage revenue had tripled to $19.9 million since the same time a year ago and the company was ahead of Women.com and Oxygen, but net loss had also doubled to $37.7 million.

Clearly seeing the profit

To expand content and services, iVillage purchased Women.com Networks Inc. for $30 million in cash and stock in February 2001, and Promotions.com, a provider of Internet promotions and e-mail marketing, in February 2002. The first deal added 100,000 pages of women-related content to the site's cache, while the second provided iVillage advertisers with direct marketing and promotional capabilities.

Next up for the company was a bit of diversification. During the summer of 2002, iVillage introduced a line of vitamins and nutraceutical supplements—including Mommy Must Have, a blend of folic acid and iron for pregnant women, and See Clearly, which contains bilberry, an antiseptic said to help the eyes—as part of a new catalog of iVillage-branded products, including makeup, bath oils and baby formula.

By pushing into the branded-product market, CEO McCormick noted the company was "making something happen" instead of idly waiting for advertisers to come knocking. iVillage relies on other manufacturers to make, store and ship the items, and receives a commission in return for promoting the products on the company's web site. Other money-making schemes included offering online seminars and workshops for a fee. One of the first such workshops was a six-week online sexual self-improvement course offered during the winter of 2002 for $35, which pulled in a cool $100,000.

User friendly

iVillage inked a deal in Rutledge Hill Press in 2003 to publish a series of books on women's issues and interests, such as cooking, dating and pregnancy. iVillage co-founder Nancy Evans called the deal an "opportunity to exchange information with a new audience." In June 2003, iVillage partnered with drugstore.com to make available the online retailer's intimacy and sexuality offerings to iVillage members, and launched its iVillage Sex Boutique to promote the products.

In April 2005, iVillage bought its iVillage.co.uk web site subsidiary and related assets from Tesco for an undisclosed amount. The same month, iVillage picked up HealthCentersOnline, a privately held online destination for physician-edited information on patient health conditions, treatments and preventative care. McCormick noted that health care information was a top concern for women visitors to iVillage. The acquisition also marked the beginning of an iVillage initiative to highlight heart disease, a top killer of women.

Growing on all accounts

For the second quarter ended June 2005, iVillage posted revenue of $21.1 million, a 28 percent increase from the year prior. Overall, though, the company reported a net loss of $0.3 million, compared to a net income of $0.1 million the year prior. iVillage continues to carry no debt, and expected to earn between $9 million and $10 million in net income for the total fiscal year 2005.

In August 2005, iVillage announced an exclusive distribution agreement with Yahoo! Search Marketing to bring Yahoo!'s search products to iVillage's 15.5 million unique monthly visitors. Yahoo! Search will replace iVillage's existing web search listings. McCormick noted search and contextual advertising were "very important growth areas" for both the Internet community and iVillage.

GETTING HIRED

Gaining entrance into the Village

Though iVillage's web site offers a wealth of career information, it's stingy when it comes to info on itself. Interested parties should send resumes and cover letters directly to the company's human resources department.

Insiders admit that the company's massive burn rate hasn't made it a stable employer. One source describes periodic layoffs where "generally one or two people are fired from each department." Still, iVillage periodically recruits personnel for its "channels." Employees add that while the majority of iVillagers are female, most of the company's technical personnel are male.

Level 3 Communications, Inc.

1025 Eldorado Boulevard
Broomfield, CO 80021
Phone: (720) 888-1000
Fax: (720) 888-5085
www.level3.com

LOCATION

Broomfield, CO (HQ)

THE STATS

Employer Type: Public Company
Stock Symbol: LVLT
Stock Exchange: NASDAQ
Chairman: Walter Scott Jr.
CEO: James Q. (Jim) Crowe
2004 Employees: 4,500
2004 Revenue ($mil.): $3,712

KEY COMPETITORS

CDW
IBM Global Services
WilTel

EMPLOYMENT CONTACT

www.level3.com/2959.html

Visit Vault at **www.vault.com** for insider company profiles, expert advice,
career message boards, expert resume reviews, the Vault Job Board and more.

VAULT CAREER LIBRARY   **137**

THE SCOOP

Bandwith behemoth

Level 3 Communications operates long-haul networks in the U.S. and Europe—overall, one of the largest communications and Internet "backbones" across the globe. The company serves telecom and Internet carriers via fiber-optic and traditional cable networks. Level 3 has local loops in 36 U.S. and European cities and its networks include 23,000 thousand miles of U.S. intercity and European cables. Clients include the world's largest telecom carriers, the top 10 U.S. Internet service providers, and the 10 largest European telecom carriers; among its offerings are Internet Protocol services, broadband transport, colocation services and patented Softswitch-based managed modem and voice services.

Low tech beginnings

Level 3 traces its beginnings back to 1985, when the company was founded as Kiewit Diversified Group, a wholly owned subsidiary of Peter Kiewit Sons Inc. The parent company, founded more than a century ago in Omaha, Neb., originally created Kiewit Diversified as a holding company for its non-construction-based businesses. Kiewit Diversified changed names to Level 3 Communications in January 1998. In March of that year, Peter Kiewit Sons spun off Level 3, which began trading on the NASDAQ National Market in April.

Rocky road

Through the late 1990s and into the new millennium, Level 3 and many of its telecom peers built huge networks, gunning to satisfy the perceived need for bandwidth capability. In 1999, for example, Level 3 logged $515 million in revenue. The next year, the company reported that sales had made a huge jump, to $1.2 billion. Eventually, though, growth slowed, and the new fiber optics and long-distance networks that these companies raced to build at such a feverish pace remained little used. The Internet bubble that popped in 2000 made a dent in data traffic as dot-coms folded at an increasing rate. Many of the telecom industry's highest fliers, including WorldCom, Winstar and Global Crossing, eventually went bankrupt. In December 2001, amid this rocky telecom climate, Level 3 sold its Asian business to Reach, an Asian telecom carrier. The assets sold include Level 3's North Asian cable system, and data centers in Tokyo and Hong Kong. The slumping economy and the malaise affecting telecom hit Level 3 in other ways. In June 2002, Level 3 made its third round of staff cuts in 14 months, laying off 200 workers. Those cuts came on top of earlier layoffs in 2001, when the company eliminated more than 1,700 positions in April and June of that year.

New deals

In January 2002, the company announced an agreement to provide dial up Internet access to SBC Internet Services, an SBC Communications subsidiary. The minimum value of the three-year pact, the companies said, comes in at $100 million. In March 2002, Level 3 acquired Corporate Software, a software marketer and reseller, for $89 million.

Buffet brings bucks

July 2002 proved to be a newsworthy month for Level 3, and one that seemed to pull the company back from the woes affecting its peers. Investment icon Warren Buffett's company, Berkshire Hathaway, along with Legg Mason and Longleaf Capital Funds, said they would invest $500 million in Level 3. The company, for its part, said it would use the money to buy competitors' businesses, focusing on purchases that would help broaden Level 3's customer base. In a hint of Level 3's search for possible deals, that same month the company made a move to acquire Williams Communications Group, a bankrupt telecom provider, for a reported price of $1.1 billion. That deal did not go through, as the telecom's former parent company, Williams (an energy company), along with Leucadia National, announced they had come up with a plan to guide Williams Communications out of bankruptcy.

Making strides

Level 3 shifted over 300 jobs to Atlanta in March 2003, following its purchase of rival Genuity Inc. for $137 million. News of the move followed a successful winter, in which the firm picked up new customer agreements with AOL Time Warner, Cablevision Systems and Verizon Communications. Gone, though, was a Genuity unit focused on managed hosting, which Level 3 sold to Computer Sciences the following month for an undisclosed amount. That fall, the firm made major transatlantic waves, increasing network capacity in Sweden and Denmark.

Back stateside, Level 3 was equally active, picking up the wholesale dial access business of ICG Communications Inc. in April 2004 for $35 million, thus significantly expanding its North American Internet dial access service. An August 2004 contract with Charter Communications further boosted Level 3 into the VoIP

Visit Vault at www.vault.com for insider company profiles, expert advice, career message boards, expert resume reviews, the Vault Job Board and more.

VAULT CAREER LIBRARY   139

market, while a five-year, $337 million contract with Northrop Grumman gave its data-networking business a lift. Level 3 had also become France Telecom's primary provider of lit broadband transport and colocation services by the end of the year.

Not in the clear yet

Despite the wheeling and dealing, Level 3's finances were still dragging from the prolonged effects of the telecom bust. At the start of 2005, the company announced it would cut 10 percent of its workforce as part of a plan to save $60 to $70 million. Meanwhile, overseas business continued to advance, as Level 3 opened up shop in the Czech Republic in an effort to reach the growing Eastern European market. In January 2005, Level 3 eliminated its (3)Tone Business, a wholesale hosted-PBX service, after numerous technical glitches and major outages, followed by the purchase of more fiber optic lines of 360networks in March 2005. As of the summer of 2005, though, things hadn't picked up yet on the financial end—Level 3 reported a second-quarter loss of $188 million in July 2005, nearly triple the $63 million loss reported the year prior.

GETTING HIRED

On the level

The company's web site lists career opportunities, as well as links to college recruiting schedules. Applicants can build a profile, check out job descriptions and submit resumes online. The company also sponsors programs for graduating students and interns; more information is available on the Level 3 site, including personal stories from former interns regarding their experiences at Level 3.

McClatchy Interactive

1101 Haynes Street; Suite 220
Raleigh, NC 27604
Phone: (919) 861-1200
Fax: (919) 861-1300
www.mcclatchyinteractive.com

LOCATIONS

Raleigh, NC (HQ)
Mississauga, Ontario

Visit Vault at **www.vault.com** for insider company profiles, expert advice, career message boards, expert resume reviews, the Vault Job Board and more.

VAULT CAREER LIBRARY   141

THE SCOOP

Information heaven

McClatchy Interactive (formerly Nando Media), one of the pioneers of web-based news offerings, published over 400 stories daily in its hey day, ranging from international and political news to sports and entertainment, and received over 3.5 million daily hits to its sites. However, as the Internet and its capabilities grew, so did McClatchy. Today, the firm provides online publishing tools for media businesses and organizations.

McClatchy Interactive's past

The idea for the company was devised and carried out by Frank Daniels III, whose family owned and operated the *Raleigh News & Observer* from 1894 to August 1995. In 1990 Daniels felt the need to computerize the newsroom, with the ultimate goal of creating the first online newspaper. The first version of his electronic publication was introduced in 1994 and consisted of news stories on a bulletin board. By the summer of that year, the paper's new media division had moved on to the World Wide Web, and its URL was chosen to reflect its origin: 'N & O' became NandO.net, one of the first electronic news sites to debut on the Web.

In August 1995, McClatchy Newspapers purchased the *News & Observer* for a whopping $373 million. Within a month, McClatchy separated *N&O* from its Internet counterpart, and created a new media company with new digs to operate autonomously. During its first eight months as a McClatchy subsidiary, Nando.net was run by Daniels, who expanded the business to include a web site design company, a hosting service for corporate web sites, a commercial web publishing tools business, and Internet service for consumer and commercial customers. However, in April 1996, Daniels was axed in favor of McClatchy's technology director, Christian Hendricks.

Letting go of the excess

Hendricks sold off all of the ancillary businesses, and revamped the news site's editorial and tech departments. In June 1998, Nando.net was renamed Nando Media, "to better reflect the company it is becoming," according to company literature. The site divided into two major sections, the *Nando Times* and the Nando Sports Server. During Hendricks' restructuring, site traffic hit an all-time low, but turned around within a year to 2.4 million hits per day, more than double its highest level before Hendricks came in. The site also brought in revenue from an impressive list of advertisers, including American Airlines, AT&T and Ford Motors, but could not turn a profit. In February 2005, Nando partnered with Pinpoint, a search engine, to add search technology to the site in an effort to increase traffic and revenue opportunities. That November, the site gave readers the choice to receive their news ad-free, for the weekly price of one dollar through its *Nando Times No-Ads Edition*.

The big switch

As the Internet became more and more integrated with daily life in the dawn of the 21st century, *Nando Times* and Nando SportServer faced increasing competition from stronger national news sites like CNN. In April 2003, the firm disbanded the two sites, stating they no longer fit the company's strategy. Nando Media continued, however, to provide content for the web sites of McClatchy-owned papers. Slowly but surely, Nando developed its product line for media publishing, including the Digital Workbench publishing system, a classified system, InSite (a turnkey online registration system), and services for community publishing, advertising management, and web hosting. In February 2005, the firm changed its name to McClatchy Interactive to better reflect the "scope of the current operation."

GETTING HIRED

Interactive job search

McClatchy Interactive posts job openings on its career site, www.mcclatchy interactive.com/portal/employment/index.html. The firms says prospective hires "should be interested in a position with a dynamic company with various positions related to Internet technologies, web publishing and sales." It also helps "if you've had experience copy editing and with computers." If you get an interview, you'll meet with the hiring manager for the position first. If you're going for a web producer, editorial position, you'll be subjected to a grammar and editing test. The process is usually "pretty relaxed," but it would be wise to bone up on your spelling and grammar before you get there.

Visit Vault at **www.vault.com** for insider company profiles, expert advice, career message boards, expert resume reviews, the Vault Job Board and more.

VAULT CAREER LIBRARY   **143**

OUR SURVEY SAYS

Letting others do the hemorrhaging

Employees call McClatchy "a people-oriented" newspaper company with a "corporate conscience." While there is "still plenty of the pressure," which is the norm for the newspaper industry, this pressure "tends to be self-directed out of a desire to excel, rather than being external pressure from overbearing management." Although McClatchy lets its employees have "plenty of room to be creative, to take risks and make mistakes," McClatchy management tends to be risk-averse. Says an insider, "McClatchy is not a 'bleeding-edge' company when it comes to investing in new ventures. They generally like to let others 'hemorrhage money' on a project and then invest in it when it has proven that it will work."

Good benefits, solid record on diversity

Our contacts laud the benefits at McClatchy, which is as "likely as not to have the best benefits of any paper in a particular area." These benefits include "a good stock purchase program and 401k program that includes company matching." Each individual division or newspaper has its own dress code and "everyone is expected to look and act in a professional manner." Its treatment of women and minorities is "progressive," with "strong diversity goals, despite a significant relaxing of pressure from the State of California." Says an insider, "I recall several cases where women were elevated to positions as publishers and executive editors, as well as minorities who have been on the track. Two of our publishers are African-Americans." A source concludes, "While I have found some companies that would pay more, I have not seen that any can offer the kind of work environment that would cause me to want to leave McClatchy."

Meetup Inc.

632 Broadway, 10th Floor
New York, NY 10012
Phone: (212) 255-7327
Fax: (212) 255-7310
www.meetup.com

LOCATION

New York, NY (HQ)

THE STATS

Employer Type: Private Company
CEO: Scott Heiferman

KEY COMPETITORS

craigslist
Evite
Friendster

EMPLOYMENT CONTACT

www.meetup.com/jobs

Visit Vault at **www.vault.com** for insider company profiles, expert advice,
career message boards, expert resume reviews, the Vault Job Board and more.

VAULT CAREER LIBRARY   **145**

THE SCOOP

Meet me in St. Louis...or Shanghai...or Skagaströnd...

Meetup is on a quest to bring communities back together via the Internet. The company's web site, Meetup.com, allows denizens to self-organize gatherings based upon common interest, whether it be Francophilia, Italian food, Elvis Presley or scrapbooking. "Meetups" take place in neighborhoods scattered across more than 50 countries. Meetup, which believes it is "possible to make a profit and make a difference," generates revenue through group membership fees, partner organizations and advertising sponsors.

Creating a neighborhood

Co-founder Scott Heiferman first dreamt up the idea of Meetup in the days following the September 11 attacks. "New York felt more like a city of neighbors than of strangers," he said in a July 2005 interview with *The Economist*. "The question I started with was: how do you start an association today? Do you need a building in Washington? No, you go online."

From its founding in June 2002 to the start of 2004, Meetup logged over 1 million people registering for monthly "meetups" covering over 3,700 topics through alliances with a diverse array of partners including Bill O'Reilly, March for Women and United Nations Foundation. The company gained a spate of publicity by enabling meetups for supporters of Senatorial, Congressional, Gubernatorial and Presidential candidates running for office in 2004—over 500 races in all—through a partnership with Capitol Advantage; the grassroots campaign for Democratic hopeful Howard Dean was particularly popular in its ability to mobilize young voters on the Web.

Paying for friends?

The once-free company began charging a monthly membership fee for people who wanted to start their own Meetup groups in April 2005 in order to turn a profit by yearend. To help organizers subsidize their groups, Meetup offers an arrangement for groups to use eBay's PayPal payment service to collect fees and conduct fundraising drives. Although many groups disappeared when Meetup went to a paid service, the company reports 15 to 20 percent growth month-over-month. There are nearly 4,600 topics in 55 countries around the world and the company reports that profitability is now closer than ever.

GETTING HIRED

Meet market

Meetup posts job openings on its career web site, www.meetup.com/jobs, featuring qualification requirements and job descriptions. Candidates are advised to submit a resume and brief cover letter to jobs@meetup.com.

Visit Vault at **www.vault.com** for insider company profiles, expert advice,
career message boards, expert resume reviews, the Vault Job Board and more.

VAULT CAREER LIBRARY   147

Mondera Inc.

MDC-SSI
45 W. 45th Street, 15th Floor
New York, NY 10036
Phone: (212) 997-9350
Toll Free: (800) MONDERA
Fax: (212) 997-9691
www.mondera.com

LOCATION

New York, NY (HQ)

DEPARTMENTS

Customer Support
Fulfillment
Marketing
Merchandising
Programming & Development

THE STATS

Employer Type: Private Company
Chairman & CEO: Fred Mouawad

KEY COMPETITORS

BlueNile.com
Ice.com
Tiffany.com

EMPLOYMENT CONTACT

www.mondera.com

THE SCOOP

All that glitters

In the crowded online jewelry market, Mondera has an edge over the competition: it's the brainchild of Fred and Pascal Mouawad, scions of a family of jewelers dating back four generations. Launched in August 1999, Mondera carries over 20,000 diamonds—the Mouawad family specialty—and also features gemstones, watches, jewelry and other luxury items, as well as services like live Q&A chat, the *24-Karat Newsletter* and the Mondera Learning Center. With backing from @Ventures and Global Investment Partners (a private fund managed by Fred Mouawad), the company garnered $13 million in first-round venture capital financing in September 1999, a large portion of which went towards a high-profile marketing campaign.

Mondera, considered by many as the online jewelry expert, has been making fine diamonds and timeless jewelry since 1999. The company has its own product development and manufacturing team and uses its own global sourcing network to offer its customers high quality jewelry directly from the source. This global edge helps distribute Mondera's products directly to consumers in the U.S. and the rest of the world through the Web. Mondera gets diamonds directly from manufacturers in New York, Antwerp, South Africa and China. Some of its jewelry is manufactured in its own state-of-the-art facilities overseas.

Diamonds are a Mouawad's best friend

The Mouawad family is one of the major players in the secretive international jewelry business. Family patriarch Robert Mouawad has bought some of the world's most famous diamonds for the family's collection, including the 70-carat Excelsior I and the 30-carat Cullinan Blue necklace. Robert's grandfather, Daoud, founded Mouawad Jewellers in his native Lebanon in 1890, and Daoud's son, Fayez moved the family business to Saudi Arabia in 1950. Robert Mouawad expanded the company aggressively in the 1960s and 1970s, building eight manufacturing operations around the world. But until his sons Pascal and Fred started Mondera, the Mouawads did little business in the U.S., choosing instead to focus on the lucrative international jewelry sector.

Visit Vault at **www.vault.com** for insider company profiles, expert advice,
career message boards, expert resume reviews, the Vault Job Board and more.

VAULT CAREER LIBRARY **149**

The gem of the 'Net

Mondera offers services comparable to a brick-and-mortar jeweler: a 30-day return policy, certified diamonds and, perhaps most importantly, advice on selecting the perfect gemstone. The Mouawads hope to use their background in the jewelry industry to leapfrog over the crowded playing field, which includes online retailers like eluxury.com, ashford.com and miadora.com. Mondera also faces stiff competition from well-known retailers like Tiffany & Co., which began offering its goods online in 2000, and New York-based Fortunoff, which sells an array of merchandise over the Internet. In response to the crowded market, Mondera rolled out a new $20 million dollar advertising campaign at the start of 2000. The same year, the company announced that it had completed a second round of financing—a $25 million fund from a group of investors including DLJ's Sprout Group. Funding was used to expand operations and to strengthen the company's brand. The company made waves in 2002 and 2003 at fashion shows sponsored by lingerie king Victoria's Secret featuring bras studded with over 2,500 carats of gemstones, personally designed by Robert Mouawad.

In 2004, Mondera entered into an agreement with Amazon.com, through which the super shopping site would sell Mondera products, in an effort to expand market reach. That July, the company earned the distinction of "Affiliate's Choice Award" from LinkShare, and, that fall, began offering free, priority shopping with its custom diamond orders.

GETTING HIRED

Enter the ring

The company's web site doesn't point to any job seeker information. Prospective employees can e-mail resumes to careers@mondera.com.

Monster Worldwide, Inc.

5 Clock Tower Place
Maynard, MA 01754
Phone: (978) 461-8000
Fax: (978) 461-8100
www.monster.com

LOCATION

Maynard, MA (HQ)

DEPARTMENTS

Monster.com
MonsterTRAK
FastWeb

THE STATS

Employer Type: Public Company
Stock Symbol: MNST
Stock Exchange: NASDAQ
Chairman & CEO: Andrew J. McKelvey
Founder and Chief Monster: Jeffrey Taylor
2005 Employees: 4,500
2004 Revenue ($mil.): $845.5

KEY COMPETITORS

CareerBuilder
HotJobs.com
Hire.com

EMPLOYMENT CONTACT

www.monsterhires.com

Visit Vault at **www.vault.com** for insider company profiles, expert advice,
career message boards, expert resume reviews, the Vault Job Board and more.

VAULT CAREER LIBRARY   151

THE SCOOP

Monster basics

Founded in 1967, Monster (formerly Monster.com) has grown to include the world's top job search web site, with more than 800,000 job listings and 34 million resumes. In addition to job ads, the site, which boasts 18 million unique visits per month, also offers career information tips on topics such as resume writing, interviewing and salary negotiation and industry-specific advice. While most of these services are free to the job seeker, Monster also has premium services—resume writing and distribution—for a fee.

Monster boasts two other web sites, in addition to monster.com, which is geared toward entry and mid-career level positions. Monster's FastWeb service allows high school students to research colleges and universities and search for scholarships. MonsterTRAK is geared toward college students and recent alumni, and is used by some 2,800 educational institutions.

Tickle me Monster

Acquired in May 2004, Tickle.com expands Monster's portfolio of services to include personality testing services. The company's best selling products, career assessment testing and social networking subscriptions, also include IQ, inkblot and talent tests. Unrelated to job search, Tickle offers a host of quizzes pertaining to entertainment and celebrities, dating and relationships, lifestyle, mind and body, teens and more.

Monster breaks out

Historically, Monster focused on large businesses and corporations. In recent years, however, the company has expanded its reach to include government organizations and small to medium-sized businesses that operate in local and regional markets. To this end, in 2004, Monster increased its sales force by around 500 and launched local market advertising campaigns in the 28 most populated U.S. cities. Adding to its government capabilities, Monster bought Military Advantage in March 2004.

The company has also bolstered its presence abroad with a number of key acquisitions. Monster snatched up German site jobpilot GmbH in April 2004 and Webneuron Services Limited, owner of India-based jobsahead.com, in June. In February 2005, the job search engine acquired a 40 percent stake in ChineHR.com and bought France's Emailjob.com. Today, the company offers 26 local language and content web sites in North America, Europe and Asia Pacific.

Monster threat?

In 2004, Monster, the jobsite, reported a $594 million revenue, up 44 percent from 2003, $413 million, and accounting for more than 70 percent of revenue for parent company Monster Worldwide. But new companies may shake things up for the established job search engine by connecting people scanning blogs for matching criteria. This direct employer to employee matching could affect the need for job sites such as Monster.com.

GETTING HIRED

Monster hires

Individuals interested in working for Monster would do well to check out the company's employment page at www.monsterhires.com. The site includes a search engine for job openings (at both Monster and parent company Monster Worldwide) as well as information about the company, sales careers, benefits and culture. According to the company, the culture "is all about being first, being fast and being out front."

MP3.com

235 Second Street
San Francisco, CA 94105
Phone: (415) 344-2000
Fax: (415) 395-9207
www.mp3.com

LOCATION

San Francisco, CA (HQ)

THE STATS

Employer Type: Subsidiary of CNET
Networks
Site Director: Laura Hess

KEY COMPETITORS

Alliance Entertainment
Amazon.com
Yahoo!

EMPLOYMENT CONTACT

www.cnetnetworks.com/careers/?tag
=mp3.ft.no

THE SCOOP

Free music!

Cashing in on the MPEG Layer 3 technology known to Internet-savvy music fans as MP3, Michael Robertson founded MP3.com in March 1998. The Internet music portal enabled web surfers to search, sample and digitally download music by utilizing MP3 technology—an audio compression technique that allows music files to be easily passed around and downloaded from the Net. Robertson's massive Internet infiltration of the music industry made quite a splash—MP3.com's initial public offering, at $28 per share, raised $361 million in net proceeds. Today, the company, which once offered free downloads for 750,000 songs from 250,000 artists, is owned by CNET Networks, and has refashioned itself as more a source of music information than actual songs following a string of devastating copyright infringement lawsuits from record labels during the late 1990s and early 2000s.

A few unknowns later ...

By starting at the grassroots level with a broad base of unsigned artists, MP3.com was able to foster the expansion of the digital music industry during the waning years of the 20th century. Offering perks for participating artists that included 50 percent returns on CD sales, no binding contracts and stock options for lucky pre-IPO participants, MP3.com quickly amassed a database of over 346,000 songs by over 56,000 artists (most of them unknown)—purportedly the then-largest collection of digital music available on the Internet.

Robertson quickly staked a major claim in the rapidly-growing market. The music industry, with its long-established structure and binding contracts, was one that must be penetrated from the bottom up, according to Robertson's business approach—one which the music maven hoped would fundamentally change the structure of the industry. Change the industry he did. But not quite in the direction he had imagined.

MP3's empire under fire

In April 1999, PlayMedia Systems, Inc., a leading developer of MP3 software technology, named MP3.com as a co-defendent in its suit against Nullsoft, Inc., developer of the "Winamp" MP3 Internet music player. PlayMedia, claiming that commercial usage of its "AMP" MP3 decoding engine requires a license, allegedly found MP3.com to be the largest redistributor of its AMP decompressors, and filed a

Visit Vault at **www.vault.com** for insider company profiles, expert advice, career message boards, expert resume reviews, the Vault Job Board and more.

VAULT CAREER LIBRARY   **155**

lawsuit for more than $15 million. PlayMedia's estimated damages, based on the number of Winamp players that MP3.com distributed, date back to April 1998.

A year later, more bad news: a federal judge found MP3.com guilty of copyright infringement in a landmark lawsuit brought against it by five major record labels—as well as artists Metallica and Dr. Dre. The judge found that since MP3 made unauthorized copies of 45,000 compact discs, loaded them onto computer servers and permitted its customers to download the music without consent from the record labels or the artist, the company was liable. MP3 was forced to close up shop on its file sharing in a May 2000 court order agreement. In October 2000, the National Music Publishers Association reached a licensing agreement with MP3.com, permitting the site to distribute digital music files. A month later, the last of its major lawsuits with the industry's Big Five record companies was settled for $53.4 million. All in all, the suits forced the site to shell out $170 million for legal costs.

The hits just keep on coming

With its major suits settled, MP3's Internet store was back in business—but not for long. Just when things seemed settled, Unity Entertainment, EMusic and a number of other independent labels filed a class-action copyright infringement complaint against MP3.com. With all of the digital drama, MP3.com reported a fourth-quarter loss to end the fiscal year 2000, though the loss of $3.1 million was narrower than Wall Street analysts anticipated.

In April 2001, MP3.com was forced to pay $296,873 to independent music label Tee Vee Toons in yet another copyright infringement case. A month later, recording artists Tom Waits and Randy Newman, and rock band Heart filed a lawsuit against the beleaguered dot-com, accusing MP3.com of wrongly copying hundreds of songs onto its site.

At the same time, Vivendi Universal, a one-time foe in the courtroom, acquired MP3.com for $372 million to boost its digital music service. The support of one of the world's largest music companies did little to ward off litigation. In June 2001, Major Bob Music, a Nashville-based publishing house, became one of the first music publishing houses to take MP3.com to court, claiming—what else?—copyright infringement.

Not your parents' MP3.com

CNET Networks, an interactive content firm based in San Francisco, purchased the URL MP3.com only from Vivendi in late 2003. The company says it wasn't offered nor did it want to buy the database of music due to the digital management issues involved. But it wanted to leverage the already popular URL to create a resource for music lovers where they could get information on their favorite music artists. The new site, which debuted in 2004, billed itself as a "comprehensive online music resource" and featured a section through which users can create a profile, track their favorite artists, write their own reviews and discuss music on MP3.com message boards.

Today's MP3.com offers streaming of the latest albums and music videos, mostly by Top 40 stars—as well as independent artists. Other features include biographies of music genres and artists, critics' reviews of albums, Billboard music charts and song downloading (for a price, naturally) via Napster, AudioLunchbox, iTunes, RealPlayer and Musicmatch. Whole CDs are also available for purchase through a partnership with mySimon.com, also owned by CNET.

GETTING HIRED

C you there

MP3.com does not list specific jobs at the company. Instead, check parent company CNET's listings at www.cnetnetworks.com/careers/?tag=mp3.ft.no.

Visit Vault at **www.vault.com** for insider company profiles, expert advice, career message boards, expert resume reviews, the Vault Job Board and more.

VAULT CAREER LIBRARY   **157**

Netflix, Inc.

970 University Avenue
Los Gatos, CA 95032
Phone: (408) 317-3700
Fax: (408) 317-3737
www.netflix.com

LOCATION

Los Gatos, CA (HQ)

THE STATS

Employer Type: Public Company
Stock Symbol: NFLX
Stock Exchange: NASDAQ
Chairman & CEO: Reed Hastings
2004 Employees: 940
2004 Revenue ($mil.): $506.2

KEY COMPETITORS

Blockbuster
Hastings Entertainment
Movie Gallery

EMPLOYMENT CONTACT

www.netflix.com/Jobs?hnjr = 8

THE SCOOP

Movie night, every night

Netflix delivers DVDs, television shows and how-to videos straight to your doorstep. The firm's web site, Netflix.com, offers over 50,000 titles for a monthly fee ($9.99 for the cheapest package, $47.99 for the most expensive; $17.99 is the most popular plan). Netflix subscribers—3.6 million strong—can order as many DVDs as they want, with no due dates or late fees. Netflix will even pay the postage. The company runs 37 distribution centers across major U.S. cities to ensure flicks are delivered in a reasonable time frame, usually within one business day of shipment.

Late fees, be gone!

Founder Reed Hastings, who previously cut his teeth in the computer world as founder and CEO of Pure Software (ranked among the world's top 50 largest public software companies before it was acquired by Rational Software), developed what would become Netflix from his own personal experience with a nuisance plaguing many cinephiles—late fees. In 1997, the former computer scientist amassed a whopping $40 in Blockbuster charges for a six-week late VHS copy of *Apollo 13*, and vowed to never let such an event happen again. At the same time, a friend introduced Hastings to the DVD format, a blossoming technology just hitting the market in the mid-1990s. Hastings had actually toyed with the idea of a mail-order VHS service in 1996, but ultimately decided the tapes were too fragile and bulky to ship. DVDs, on the other hand, could be mailed at a higher volume for a cheaper cost. An idea was born.

The sky's the limit

Hastings and his colleagues then developed a plan for a new venture they called Netflix. The company began its subscriptions service in 1999, offering an early version of its now-famous DVD rental service for $4 per movie. Despite the free shipping, the public was unimpressed with the rate-per-movie, and few subscribers came back to use the service again. Enter Hastings' "a-ha" moment: on the way to his health club one night, he had an epiphany. If his gym could offer unlimited workouts for a monthly fee, why couldn't Netflix offer unlimited movies? He went back to the drawing board, crafted a new business model based on an unlimited service and set a subscription fee at $20.

Within the first three months, Netflix boasted 100,000 subscribers, and continued to expand each quarter. An IPO in May 2002 proved successful, raising cash and boosting the firm's market cap to $750 million. By the start of 2003, the firm hit one million subscribers. That summer, Netflix picked up a patent covering many of its basic features of its business model as rivals Blockbuster and Wal-Mart quietly began developing their own DVD-mail-order services. When the two companies finally did release rental services, they operated nearly identically to Netflix—and undercut the company's subscription price.

Taking the plunge

Hastings acknowledged that the threat from Blockbuster was "serious" but was confident his firm's years of experience, good name and operational efficiency (shipping nearly one million movies on a daily basis) would fend off foes. At first, Netflix had little reason to worry—in the quarter ended July 2004, revenue had nearly doubled from $270 million the year prior to $525 million. That October, Netflix and TiVo even formed a partnership to develop technology and work with Hollywood studios to secure content for digital distribution, the first step in next-generation movie viewing, as a means of further distancing itself from the competition.

The same month, though, Netflix lowered its prices, despite Hastings' previous insistence that the price premium of $21.99 per month was necessary to keep the company growing. However, with cheaper services from rivals threatening to siphon away potential customers, Netflix had no choice. Hastings admitted the cut was necessary to stay competitive, and predicted the firm would see lower profits in the short term as a result, but spark a rise in value in the long run. To this end, the company planned to cut earnings growth for 2005, and spend more money on customer acquisition. The formula did not bode well with investors. Stock took a beating on the news, slipping 40 percent, as analysts downgraded the company's shares.

A blockbuster battle

As part of its promise to bring more value to subscribers, Netflix developed a new service, Netflix Friends, in December 2004, which let users share movie reviews and recommendations directly and automatically with friends via the company's web site, adding a social networking "movie community" aspect to the company that users appreciated. Industry bonuses and exclusives, such as mailing *The Incredibles* to subscribers the first day it was released by Pixar, also piqued user interest. By March 2005, Netflix had 2.6 million total members and record revenue of $143.9 million.

Then, in a surprising move, Wal-Mart dropped out of the rental business in May 2005 to concentrate on in-store sales, but not before offering former foe Netflix a major boost. As part of a mutual agreement between the two companies, Wal-Mart gave subscribers the opportunity to sign with Netflix at their discounted monthly subscription price of $12.97, while Netflix agreed to promote Wal-Mart's DVD sales to its subscribers. In one fell swoop, Netflix had done what scores of others could not do—upend the retail mecca. Blockbuster quickly pounced, offering new subscribers two months of free service, while tacking on coupons for use in its brick-and-mortar stores—something Netflix can't offer. In 2006, Blockbuster plans to increase its distribution centers by as much as 15,000 percent by inviting local stores to become DVD mailing centers.

Setting the stage for the digital age

Technological advancements have also forced Netflix to reexamine its business model — but in a progressive way. The company embraces the dawn of electronic delivery and digital downloading, and plans to offer services in the future that allow consumers to download movies and order standard DVDs on a single subscription based on personal preference. "It's why we called the company Netflix and not DVD by Mail," Hastings said in an August 2004 interview with *BusinessWeek* magazine. "We intend to grow to a very large DVD business, then expand and win in the downloading space."

Meanwhile, in the company's most recent quarter posted October 2005, third-quarter revenue rose 23 percent over the prior year, and new subscribers increased 61 percent year over year. Overall for the fiscal year, Netflix expects to generate over $684 million in revenue in 2005.

GETTING HIRED

The bright lights beckon

Jobs listings and descriptions are posted on the Netflix career site, www.netflix.com/Jobs. In addition, resumes can be e-mailed to greatpeople@netflix.com. Unless otherwise noted, all positions are at the company's

Visit Vault at **www.vault.com** for insider company profiles, expert advice, career message boards, expert resume reviews, the Vault Job Board and more.

VAULT CAREER LIBRARY   **161**

headquarters in Los Gatos, which has some definite perks—headquarter employees are often shuffled off to the Sundance Film Festival and Hollywood to "drink up film culture."

Open Text Corporation

185 Columbia Street West
Waterloo, Ontario N2L 5Z5, Canada
Phone: (519) 888-7111
Fax: (519) 888-0677
www.opentext.com

LOCATIONS

**Waterloo, Ontario, Canada
(Corporate HQ)
Lincolnshire, IL (Global HQ)
Grasbrunn, Germany (European HQ)**
Boston, MA
Dubai
Pyrmont, NSW, Australia

THE STATS

Employer Type: Public Company
Stock Symbol: OTEX
Stock Exchange: NASDAQ
Chairman: P. Thomas (Tom) Jenkins
CEO: John Shackleton
2004 Employees: 2,105
2004 Revenue ($mil.): $291.1

KEY COMPETITORS

FileNet
Hummingbird
Lotus

EMPLOYMENT CONTACT

www.opentext.com/corporate/careers
/index.html

Visit Vault at **www.vault.com** for insider company profiles, expert advice,
career message boards, expert resume reviews, the Vault Job Board and more.

VAULT CAREER LIBRARY   163

THE SCOOP

Software for a superfilter

Open Text delivers the ultimate in high tech applications for information junkies. It makes Intranet software that allows people to find information on any topic, from anywhere in the world; it also lets users store vast amounts of information, collaborate on projects efficiently, and share their knowledge with private and corporate networks that use the Internet. Open Text Index, the company's primary product, sorts information on the Web by indexing every word on a page instead of only key words. Big-name clients include IBM, AT&T and the BBC. More than 4,000 companies use its Livelink product; other offerings include software for managing collections of cataloged information (BASIS), library automation (Techlib), and group scheduling (OnTime).

A sieve for the ocean

The firm was founded by computer scientist Tim Bray and two of his colleagues from the University of Waterloo. In 1987 they began working on an electronic system to store and catalog the Oxford English Dictionary, which they completed in 1989. They launched the company in 1991. Its flagship product at the time was a text-searching application for document retrieval. Bray soon found that niche too small, so in 1994, he set the company's sights on developing organizational software for the World Wide Web. In 1995 the company introduced Open Text Index, an application thorough enough to apply to the vast amount of data on the Internet.

Working from the outside in

Later that year the firm decided to target business consumers by applying its indexing technology to project management software for corporate intranets. Having finally found the perfect niche, Open Text chose to cement its place in the market by acquiring competitors. It bought software makers Internet Anywhere and Intunix, which had developed an information search product that was combined with Open Text 5 for PC hard drive and CD-ROM searches. With the purchase of a company called Odesta came ownership of the remarkably successful Livelink software, as well as a number of strategic partnerships with information technology firms. The Livelink application is now used on OT's "Livelink Pinstripe" site—a search tool targeted to business users. It makes information gathering more efficient, as it only indexes sites useful to businesspeople.

Upward and onward

Open Text went public in 1996, and the next year it forged an agreement to bundle Livelink with Netscape's SuiteSpot server software. It also worked jointly with Hewlett-Packard to develop a web-based intranet application for network PCs. In summer 1998, the firm acquired software maker Information Dimensions, Inc.—its ninth acquisition. IDI software is used to manage internal corporate data and communications, like e-mail and scheduling systems. The merger gave Open Text a much larger presence in Europe and a combined 42.7 percent market share in the worldwide enterprise-document market. Growth in 1998 was further promoted by big account wins from blue chip clients including CVS drug stores and computer maker Silicon Graphics. In 1999 the company acquired Canadian software maker Lava Systems; it purchased PSSoftware Solutions to augment its records management; it formed an alliance with J.D. Edwards; and it purchased a stake in Communities.com, producer of instant messaging and conferencing applications.

Tragedy averted

After going through an unsuccessful hostile takeover bid of rival PC Docs, a $170 million lawsuit filed by competitor NetSys Technology Group and poor financial reports in late-1999, Open Text's unbridled success appeared to be over, despite its numerous acquisitions. Rumors of its imminent takeover spread. However, the company's 1999 annual report and subsequent quarterly reports demonstrated a significant recovery, and in April 2000, Open Text won its arbitration with NetSys. The company had charged Open Text with breach of contract and with negligent misrepresentation. Two months earlier, the unveiling of two new Open Text programs—myLiveLink and b2bScene.com—resulted in soaring stock prices. Other 2000 accomplishments include an alliance with fellow Waterloo resident Research in Motion Ltd.; a pact with Euopean Internet provider KPNQwest; and a partnership with Cabrian Resources' ServicePoint, an e-business site.

International shopping spree

In the six months between September 2002 and March 2003, Open Text completed a series of deals to expand its software services; e-mail, voicemail and fax message management; and portal software framework, picking up Centrintiny Inc., a unified messaging software developer; Eloquent Inc., developer of collaboration add-ons to sales force automation application; and Corechange, Inc. for a total of roughly $30 million.

Visit Vault at **www.vault.com** for insider company profiles, expert advice, career message boards, expert resume reviews, the Vault Job Board and more.

VAULT CAREER LIBRARY   165

Next up were back-to-back purchases of German companies as part of a plan to expand Open Text's international presence. In August 2003, the firm purchased content management software developer Gauss Interprise for $11 million, adding 1,000 new global customers, followed by IXOS Software AG, which brought content management and archiving software into the Open Text fold. The buys helped lift Open Text's net revenue to $177.7 million, from $154.4 million the year prior, for the fiscal year 2003.

The split

Following the German acquisitions, Open Text announced a massive restructuring plan, which would divide the company into two divisions. The first, its North American division, would have operational headquarters in the suburbs of Chicago, and would be in charge of both collaboration and knowledge management solutions on a global scale, and North American operations. The other division, European-based, would be headquartered in the Munich area, with global responsibility for content management and archiving, as well as European responsibility for operations. For the fiscal year 2004, Open Text reported revenue of $291.1 million, up 64 percent from the year prior, a record for the company. Second quarter revenue posted in February 2005 revealed a profit of $114.7 million, the highest in company history. That July, John Shackleton, a longtime employee of Open Text, was promoted to CEO, replacing Tom Jenkins, who remained as chairman of the board.

For all of the wheeling and dealing, Wall Street was unimpressed. Analysts downgraded shares of Open Text to Hold from Buy in July 2005, expressing concern that the firm was "excessively enthusiastic" about growth potential in the market, and citing "unreliable internal forecasting" and "ongoing restructuring" leading to "great uncertainity" over how the company would be able to manage expectations in upcoming quarters.

GETTING HIRED

Opening the door

Current job openings are posted in the career opportunities section of the Open Text web site. The company also recruits at job fairs and on college campuses. To apply for a position, include the job title along with your resume and cover letter. If you are applying for more than one position, list all of the appropriate job titles in your cover letter. Resumes may be faxed or sent by regular mail to the human resources department at either office listed. You can also e-mail resumes and cover letters in Microsoft Word, ASCII or HTML format to careers@opentext.com. The human resources department does not accept phone calls.

Sources say that there are usually more positions open than are listed, so send a resume even if you don't see the perfect description on the site. Interviews are quite relaxed but occasionally long. One employee reports meeting with six people in three interviews before receiving an offer. In general, though, candidates must only endure two rounds.

OUR SURVEY SAYS

Friendly, but not too friendly

The Open Text HQ is set in idyllic surroundings, so on lunch breaks, employees get to stroll through a Japanese garden complete with ponds, ducks, swans and a walking trail. It's not surprising that despite the fast-moving atmosphere, work doesn't feel like a grind. Instead, Open Text boasts a very flexible environment and the company is rapidly expanding, so things are quite exciting right now. Sources say "Open Text is a very virtual company" and note that "it's kind of hard to have a corporate culture when we are so spread out." Employees in different offices communicate a great deal via conference calls and e-mail. In addition, many in programming and development telecommute or work on their own flex-time schedules. Workers who go to the office every day get along well, but most aren't interested in socializing too much after hours.

There's no dress code unless you are regularly meeting with customers, and many employees wear shorts in the summer. "Salaries are satisfactory," according to at least one source, and "you can afford to have a social life." And employees have plenty of time to enjoy themselves, since most departments don't require much overtime. There are quite a few minority employees and a number of women across the board. The employees are said to be highly intelligent, top-notch programmers, and the work is not stressful so much as it is fast-paced. "You have to be bright and very good at what you do," comments one insider, "otherwise people are not going to have patience with you."

In addition to non-matching 401(k) and medical coverage, employees benefit from good stock option and stock purchase plans. There are always some growing pains with a rapidly expanding company in a highly competitive field, but Open Text sources maintain that any such difficulties have not been unmanageable.

Orbitz, LLC

200 S. Wacker Drive
Suite 1900
Chicago, IL 60606
Phone: (312) 894-5000
Fax: (312) 894-5001
www.orbitz.com

LOCATION

Chicago, IL (HQ)

DEPARTMENTS

Corporate Travel
Orbitz.com

THE STATS

Employer Type: Subsidiary of Cendant
President and CEO: Mitch Truwit
2004 Employees: 400
2003 Revenue ($ mil): $241.8

KEY COMPETITORS

Expedia
Priceline
Travelocity

EMPLOYMENT CONTACT

E-mail: resume@orbitz.com

Visit Vault at **www.vault.com** for insider company profiles, expert advice,
career message boards, expert resume reviews, the Vault Job Board and more.

VAULT CAREER LIBRARY   169

THE SCOOP

Airfares and more

Orbitz knows airplane tickets—and it should. The No. 3 online travel agency was founded by five airlines—American, Continental, Northwest and United Airlines—to keep pace with Travelocity and others in the online reservation and tickets sales industry.

These days, Orbitz isn't just limited to airlines; the company also offers deals on hotels, rental cars, cruises and vacation packages. The site's easy-to-use format and matrix display have earned the company numerous awards, including *Travel Savvy*'s Best web site for booking travel in September/October 2004, *PC Magazine*'s Editor's Choice Award in April 2004 and Forbes.com's #1 Travel Site in August 2003.

Originally controlled by the founding five, Orbitz went public in 2003, but was snatched up by Cendant Corporation in September 2004 for $1.25 billion. Today, Orbitz is a wholly owned subsidiary of Cendant and a division of the firm's Travel Distribution Services unit (which includes other travel sites such as CheapTickets.com, RatesToGo.com and the Away Network).

A long way from the top

With 17 percent of the online travel market share in 2004 (compared to Travelocity's 20 percent and Expedia's 40 percent), Orbitz has certainly earned itself a spot among the Big Three—especially considering the company didn't launch its web site to the public until June 2001. On the flip side, an August 2004 *BusinessWeek* article described Orbitz as "the problem child of the group." At the time, roughly 25 percent of the rooms Orbitz sold were high-profit merchant rooms—meaning Orbitz bought rooms from the hotels and then marked them up for resale, rather than serving as a middle man for a small commission. In comparison, 90 percent of the rooms IAC (Expedia's parent company) sold fell into this category.

The company's acquisition by Cendant may be just the pick-me-up Orbitz needs. The company should benefit from Cendant's ownership of hotel chains such as Howard Johnson and the Ramada Inn, and car rental companies Avis and Budget. Looked at another way, Orbitz may be just the pick-me-up Cendant needs, boosting sales of its hotel and car rental brands.

GETTING HIRED

Work hard, play hard

Orbitz boasts business casual dress, a state-of-the-art office environment and discounted health club membership as just a few of the perks of working for the online travel agency. The company also offers a "competitive salary" and "comprehensive array of employee benefit programs." The overall message seems to be "work hard, play hard."

If this sounds like the place for you, check out the current list of available positions (see the "careers" section at the bottom of the main web site) or send your resume to resume@orbitz.com.

Visit Vault at **www.vault.com** for insider company profiles, expert advice,
career message boards, expert resume reviews, the Vault Job Board and more.

VAULT CAREER LIBRARY   **171**

Organic, Inc.

555 Market Street, 4th Floor
San Francisco, CA 94105
Phone: (415) 581-5300
Fax: (415) 581-5400
www.organic.com

LOCATIONS

San Francisco, CA (HQ)
Detroit, MI
Los Angeles, CA
New York, NY
Toronto

DEPARTMENTS

Experience Design
Interactive Marketing
Measurement and Analytics
Site Operations and Outsourcing
Usability Testing
Web Strategy
Web Technology and
  Implementation

THE STATS

Employer Type: Subsidiary of
Omnicom
Chairman: Jonathan Nelson
CEO: Mark Kingdon
2004 Employees: 250
2004 Revenue ($mil.): $52.0

KEY COMPETITORS

aQuantive
Critical Mass
Digitas

EMPLOYMENT CONTACT

E-mail: resumes@organic.com

THE SCOOP

Before the e-boom

When Organic, Inc. made its debut in 1993, the Internet was just a shadow of what it is today. The San Francisco-based web development and marketing company quickly made a name for itself as a pioneer in the industry, developing some of the first corporate sites on the Web and launching the first online advertising banner. Founded before the e-boom, Organic survived the e-bust through continued innovation in its field. In 2003, the web developer was snatched up by communications conglomerate Omnicom.

Today, the company is small, with around 250 employees working out of offices in Detroit, Los Angeles, New York, San Francisco and Toronto, but still vital. To date, Organic has delivered more than 750 engagements to clients in five key industry groups: automotive, financial services, retail, technology and communications. Services include web strategy, experience design, web technology and implementation, usability testing, measurement and analytics, interactive marketing, and site operations and outsourcing.

(Web) Site seeing

Organic was the first business dedicated to building commercial web sites, and www.organic.com was one of the first 100 sites to appear on the Internet. In 1994, Organic developed the first sites for illustrious clients like AT&T, MCI, Volvo, Saturn and Club Med. The company then created Apache, the most widely distributed software server in the world, and gained a 63 percent market share. The web developer helped build the first online version of *Wired* magazine, hotwired.com, which also featured the first banner ad. Organic went on to develop Accrue, a new tool for web site measurement and analysis in 1995. In the same year, Organic introduced strategic consulting services that launched ventures for brands such as Riven, as well as the *Star Wars* site. The following year, the company developed Nike's web site for the Atlanta Summer Olympics. In 1998, Organic invested in start-ups while building sites for brands like Chase, Zagat Survey and Corbis. Organic also co-branded the *Consumer Online Commerce Report* with Cyber Dialogue to create an in-depth report used to analyze e-commerce market trends that year. In 2002, the web developer was first in the industry to develop a wireless application protocol for a client's site.

Visit Vault at **www.vault.com** for insider company profiles, expert advice, career message boards, expert resume reviews, the Vault Job Board and more.

VAULT CAREER LIBRARY   **173**

In 2003, Domino's Pizza announced the launch of a new bilingual feature on www.dominos.com, created by Organic. The move made Domino's the first national pizza delivery company to offer the majority of its U.S. web site in Spanish. That year, Organic added William Sonoma, Armani Exchange, Benjamin Moore, President's Choice and the Royal Bank of Canada to its list of clients. In 2004, the company won an account with US Airways, helped Raymond James launch its web site, redesigned Fannie Mae's site and launched the Jeep 4x4 Trail Rated Challenge.

Creating an "exceptional experience"

Organic works with new clients to establish a "relationship charter," an agreement defining mutual expectations, roles and performance measures. The company's goal is to help clients create an exceptional online experience for their customers. Whether Internet, extranet or intranet, Organic, Inc. believes that a site must be executed, measured and constantly improved. The web developer has six criteria for its "Mark of Exceptional Experience." Exceptional web sites recognize needs, see relationships holistically, revel in the details, showcase the brand, evolve continually and easily, and are profitable.

How to stay on top

Winning is nothing new for Organic. In 2005 alone, the company won 21 Internet Advertising Competition (IAC) awards for its work with the Chrysler Group, Tommy Hilfiger, Seiko, Benjamin Moore, 20th Century Fox, Sprint and SIRIUS Satellite Radio, and two Macromedia "Site of the Day" awards for Dodge Charger "Unleash Your Freak" and the Chrysler PT Cruiser Customizer. In May 2005, the Web Marketing Association recognized Organic, Inc. as the Top Agency of 2005.

GETTING HIRED

EEE for the WWW

Organic, Inc. lists its current openings on the career section of its web site. Postings include a complete job description as well as a list of skills and qualifications. Interested candidates should submit a cover letter and resume to resumes@organic.com. An important part of the hiring process for Organic is the Exceptional Experience Essay. All applicants must write a short essay on an exceptional experience, such as loading your Apple iPod with 1980's disco music from iTunes or finding a rare book on Amazon.com with just three clicks of the mouse. The essay form can be downloaded online and should be e-mailed to EEessays@organic.com.

Visit Vault at **www.vault.com** for insider company profiles, expert advice, career message boards, expert resume reviews, the Vault Job Board and more.

V/\ULT CAREER LIBRARY   175

PCQuote.com

155 Spring Street, 3rd Floor
New York, NY 10012
Phone: (212) 334-2000
Fax: (212) 334-4464
www.pcquote.com

LOCATIONS

New York, NY (HQ)
Forked River, NJ

THE STATS

Employer Type: Subsidiary of
Money.net
CEO (Money.net): Harold L. (H.L.)
Van Arnem

KEY COMPETITORS

America Online
MarketWatch
Yahoo!

EMPLOYMENT CONTACT

E-mail: corporate@money.net

THE SCOOP

It's the Information Age

Through advanced satellite technology, PCQuote supplies financial market data to brokerages, fund managers, banks, investors and consumers, and also provides real-time data for professionals through subscription services MarketSmart and MarketScreen. The company was founded as On-Line Response in 1975 by options traders, with primarily institutional financial services firms (banks and money managers) as its clients; its first product was a real-time option analysis system. Renamed PCQuote in 1983, the company spent the 1980s on product development, which ultimately left profits low until a cost-cutting campaign paired up with new big-name contracts in 1994, bringing earnings to a record $1.5 million in 1995.

It's not about PCs; it's about the Net

Revenue from Internet services proved a valuable source of profit, growing from 6 percent of company revenue in 1996 to nearly 30 percent the year after, with subscriptions to PCQuote services rounding out the rest of the firm's income. In the late 1990s, the company's web site, pcquote.com, averaged 34 million page views each month (and close to 1 million visitors). By December 1998, the company had created an Internet division to focus on its web strategy; in February 1999, PC Quote unveiled a redesign of its site. Unlike competitors, PCQuote let users slice and dice its data, using its own software or third party software. The company also offered its services through its site on the World Wide Web and through the Microsoft Network and other online content providers, and signed an agreement with Schaeffer's Investment Research to provide real-time information on options. In an effort to expand the appeal of its products, PCQuote released PCQuote Orbit, a scaled-down version of its professional software intended for the individual investor.

In the money

For all of the Internet advancements, PCQuote was unable to eclipse its million-dollar days of the mid-1990s, losing money each consecutive year following 1995. The American Stock Exchange briefly halted trading of PCQuote shares in April 1998 after the company reported a net loss of $2.7 million for its fourth quarter. The firm was forced to postpone a planned IPO in March 2000, plagued by continued financial troubles and "unfavorable market conditions." Parent company HyperFeed sold off PCQuote's web site and trading applications to Money.net, a financial

Visit Vault at www.vault.com for insider company profiles, expert advice, career message boards, expert resume reviews, the Vault Job Board and more.

VAULT CAREER LIBRARY   177

services provider, in June 2003, as part of a plan to decrease "the overhead of servicing retail-based customers." A month later, the rest of PCQuote's holdings were sold to Tribal Fusion, which owned Money.net.

GETTING HIRED

Unquotable

PCQuote does not provide any job information on its web site. Send a query to parent company Money.net at corporate@money.net.

OUR SURVEY SAYS

"Cool" environment

Described as "a pretty cool place to work," employees praise PCQuote's friendly environment. The relaxed atmosphere starts with the company's dress code. Explains one insider, "Dress code is business casual, but other than the executives, a lot of people stretch that to jeans without any problem." According to another, "Everyone up to Jim Porter, the CEO, is on a first-name basis, so it's a really nice atmosphere."

The loose atmosphere isn't just a culture thing: it impacts the work at PCQuote. Explains one insider, "It's not unusual for small companies to be a bit less organized but that can also translate into a lot of opportunities to stretch the job description a bit."

Great diversity

Insiders at PCQuote also give their employers high marks when it comes to diversity issues. According to one, "The majority of our employees are female, and we all come from a variety of backgrounds." Another longtime employee agrees that "we've certainly got a very diverse mix of people working here." And yet another contact, a former employee, reports that "my boss was a woman, and many key positions in sales, PR, marketing and product management are held by women." Still, one employee notes that many management-level employees "tend to come from the old boy's network, or are the old boy's female friends."

PCQuote insiders report some points of discontent. One employee reports a high turnover rate in some departments, "though sales and advertising tend to be more stable." And with the company's poor fiscal performance in recent years, employees say that "money's not exactly something they're throwing around, but things are definitely not as bad as they had been." However, in addition to competitive pay, employees say benefits are "better than at most places." Sums up one longtime worker, "In general, it's a pretty good place to work."

Visit Vault at **www.vault.com** for insider company profiles, expert advice, career message boards, expert resume reviews, the Vault Job Board and more.

VAULT CAREER LIBRARY   179

Priceline.com

800 Connecticut Avenue
Norwalk, CT 06854
Phone: (203) 299-8000
Fax: (203) 299-8948
www.priceline.com

LOCATION

Norwalk, CT (HQ)

DEPARTMENTS

Financial Services
Travel Services

THE STATS

Employer Type: Public Company
Stock Symbol: PCLN
Stock Exchange: NASDAQ
President, CEO and Director: Jeffrey
H. Boyd
2004 Employees: 438
2004 Revenue ($mil.): $914.4

KEY COMPETITORS

Expedia
Orbitz
Travelocity

EMPLOYMENT CONTACT

www.priceline.com/jobs/default.asp

THE SCOOP

Name your price

Priceline began with a stunningly simple idea: let consumers bid on the 500,000 airplane seats that go unsold each day. When founder Jay Walker first put his idea online in April 1998, he believed his concept could usher in a new era in airline pricing. The idea caught on rapidly with flyers, particularly those seeking a cut-rate deal on last-minute travel. But, in the early days, demand far outstripped supply, with only 7 percent of bidders in 1998 actually "winning" a flight. Such problems were partially alleviated after Walker signed up his first major American carrier, Delta, in the summer of 1998. The Delta deal was the breakthrough that Walker had been waiting for: Northwest and Continental signed on almost immediately thereafter, and the company soon received an infusion of $55 million in private funds from the likes of financier George Soros and Microsoft co-founder Paul Allen. Walker also hired a couple of well-respected executives to help run the company: former Citicorp president Richard Braddock came aboard in August 1998 as chairman and CEO, and ex-AT&T exec Dan Schulman became president and COO in June 1999. (Today, the company is headed up by Jeff Boyd, who joined Priceline in January 2000 and was appointed president and CEO in November 2002).

More than just plane tickets

By mid-1999, Walker's company started expanding its product offerings, with a similar "name your price" deal on hotel rooms in over 1,000 U.S. cities. Today, customers can shop for airline tickets, hotel rooms, rental cars, vacation packages and cruises. Priceline also offers a personal finance service that includes home mortgages, refinancing and home equity loans through an independent licensee.

In addition to growing its range of product offerings, priceline.com has also branched out overseas. Outside of the United States, Priceline now owns Priceline.co.uk, a London-based online travel services, and also has a stake in an Asian travel service, also called priceline.com, which operates in Hong Kong and Singapore.

Comparison shopping

In April 2005, Priceline introduced a new twist to its traditional "Name Your Own Price" service. Now, visitors to the site can comparison shop for plane tickets, hotels, cars and more using a travel search engine allowing customers to see published prices. The move was prompted by the success of the company's retail airline tickets service, initiated in January 2004. The re-launch of priceline.com as a one-stop travel reservation site is being advertised by a multimillion dollar TV ad campaign entitled, "Shop—Compare—Save" featuring William Shatner.

Here to stay

Despite rough times for Internet companies earlier in the decade, Priceline has managed to stay in the game—and then some. In 2004, Priceline was the fastest growing of the "Big 4" online travel services (Expedia, Orbitz and Travelocity are the other three). For the year, the company reported gross travel bookings of $1.68 billion, a 52 percent increase over 2003. Revenue grew to $914.4 million from $863.7 million in the previous year and net income increased 100 percent to $38.4 million. The company attributes its impressive growth rate to the continued success of its traditional opaque travel options combined with its new retail airline tickets service. Priceline expects to see even further gains from the launch of retail options for hotel rooms, rental cars and vacation packages.

GETTING HIRED

Job line

Priceline.com advertises available job opportunities under the "jobs" section of its web site. Postings provide a description of key responsibilities, a list of required skills and qualifications, and contact information. For the position of Manager, Media Planning and Strategy, for example, the company is looking for individuals with five to seven years experience in media buying and planning, a degree in marketing and strong quantitative and analytical skills.

RealNetworks, Inc.

2601 Elliott Avenue, Suite 1000
Seattle, WA 98121
Phone: (206) 674-2700
Fax: (206) 674-2699
www.realnetworks.com

LOCATION

Seattle, WA (HQ)

THE STATS

Employer Type: Public Company
Stock Symbol: RNWK
Stock Exchange: NASDAQ
Chairman & CEO: Robert (Rob) Glaser
2004 Employees: 826
2004 Revenue ($mil.): $266.7

KEY COMPETITORS

America Online
Apple Computer
Microsoft

EMPLOYMENT CONTACT

www.realnetworks.com/company/jobs

Visit Vault at **www.vault.com** for insider company profiles, expert advice, career message boards, expert resume reviews, the Vault Job Board and more.

VAULT CAREER LIBRARY   183

THE SCOOP

A real winner

RealNetworks is a pioneer and reigning leader in the delivery and playback of streaming audio and visual programs on the Internet. The company's RealPlayer transmits programs produced by everyone from the major television networks to the U.S. Senate, Merrill Lynch and the National Football League to millions of web browsers across the world. More than 300 million people have downloaded the company's RealPlayer product, which grants access to news, sports and entertainment content through RealOne, downloadable games through RealArcade, and downloadable music through Rhapsody, RealPlayer Music Store and RadioPass. RealNetworks also develops a line of software products and services for creating, delivering and licensing digital content for the enterprise market. In addition, the RealOne SuperPass, which provides brand-name digital programming from ABCNEWS.com, CNN, FOXSports.com and NASCAR.com among others, is the fastest growing Internet paid rich media subscription service in history, with over 1 million paid subscribers.

Teaming up with the biggies

Rob Glaser left Microsoft, where he had been vice president of multimedia and consumer systems, to found RealNetworks in 1994. The next year, with the World Wide Web still in its infancy, RealNetworks (then called Progressive Networks) introduced the RealAudio system, which allowed companies to create and deliver continuous audio content through the Internet. With RealAudio, web users could back the content on demand without download delays. RN also created a system to deliver motion video.

With its RealPlayer multimedia player on 95 million computers and taking up 85 percent of the streaming media market by the late 1990s, the company teamed up with industry leaders including America Online, Macromedia, Sun Microsystems and Apple to build RealNetworks, a technological standard for the fledgling world of continuous media delivery.

In 1999 the company introduced RealJukebox, trumpeted by CEO Glaser as "the biggest breakthrough in music listening since the Walkman." The public agreed—the product reached one million downloads in 10 days. RealJukebox enabled users to play, record, organize and search for music from a single interface. Users can record

CD collections to their hard drives, personalize their collections, and then play them on their PCs or on a portable device. And in June 1999, the company launched RealSlideshow, a product in which users are able to put together photo and audio presentations that can be broadcast over the Internet.

Going broad

The next year, RealNetworks improved and broadened the process for downloading the online content that has made the company famous. In January 2000, it purchased Atlanta-based Netzip, which produces software that speeds up download times, for $268 million in stock. At the same time, it announced an upgrade in video uplink software that enables producers to send movies over the Internet that rival VCRs in picture quality. Two months later, it inked a deal to deliver broadband streaming media over satellites.

The battle lines are drawn

For all of its innovations, RealNetworks still faced a relentless competitor in Microsoft, which also hawks multimedia software. In May 2000, RealNetworks unveiled RealServer8, a streaming technology designed to deliver VHS-quality videos to users' computer screens. Microsoft said that everything available in RealServer8 was already a feature of its Windows Media Technologies 7. In a classic example of "he said, she said," RealNetworks responded that "it's a product that's a couple of generations behind us."

In May 2002, the battle heated up once again, as Microsoft and RealNetworks debated over whether RealNetworks' media player could function if Microsoft removed its media player from the Windows operating system. Not surprisingly, the spat came at a time when Microsoft overtook Real as the leading streaming media company. Microsoft claimed RealNetworks' RealOne player depended on key Windows features; RealNetworks said the player relied on operating system functions, not Windows Media, and accused Microsoft of "clearly trying to mislead the court." The issue was further compounded in December 2003, after RealNetworks sued Microsoft on antitrust charges, accusing the firm of using its Windows monopoly to "restrict how PC makers install competing media players." RealNetworks General Counsel said damages could be upwards of $1 billion. Litigation is still pending as of August 2005.

Visit Vault at **www.vault.com** for insider company profiles, expert advice, career message boards, expert resume reviews, the Vault Job Board and more.

VAULT CAREER LIBRARY   185

Straying from the desktop

As the market for computers leveled off in 2001, RealNetworks turned to other forms of technology to generate revenue and keep content diversified. A February 2001 deal with Wavefly enabled Internet video to play directly on TV, while a June, agreement with Cisco Systems, a top supplier of Internet networking equipment, integrated RealNetworks' technology into its line of content networking products. Through the deal, Cisco also agreed to sell RealNetworks' streaming media technology platform, RealSystem iQ, to enterprise customers—just as Microsoft began negotiations with America Online to provide its own streaming media technology through AOL's Internet service. In August 2003, RealNetworks announced an agreement with Sprint to offer a service allowing Sprint wireless-data customers to subscribe to news, horoscopes, traffic and other information from RealNetworks via mobile phones, marking the first time RealNetworks offered such a subscription and proving the company's larger focus to spread audio and video software from the desktop to wireless devices.

Sour apples

Always innovating, RealNetworks released a free music player in February 2004 to handle both AAC music files (used by Apple's iTunes) and WMA files (used by most other companies) as part of a strategy to capitalize on the music downloading craze. The player also featured Real's first foray into the online music store business, and offered a streaming playback system. One sore point was that the files couldn't play on Macs or on Apple's iPod. RealNetworks thus reached out to Apple to try to strike a bargain, but Apple CEO Steve Jobs refused offers by Glaser to form an online music alliance, preferring to keep the iPod Apple-only. Glaser framed his argument as a joining of forces against common "evil" Microsoft, but Jobs wasn't swayed.

To compensate, RealNetworks developed its own software, called Harmony, in June 2004, to allow users to download music from its online store and use it on any MP3 product, including the iPod. The Apple camp was furious, and slammed RealNetworks for using "the tactics and ethics of a hacker." RealNetworks countered that "consumers, and not Apple, should be the ones choosing what music goes on their iPod."

At your service

In February 2005, RealNetworks expanded a long-term relationship to enable Nokia to ship RealAudio, RealVideo and RealPlayer on a number of Nokia mobile devices.

A representative for RealNetworks called the deal "a major milestone for digital mobile media services." However, the digital music download wars rage on. Yahoo! entered the online subscription battlefield in May 2005, in an announcement that sent RealNetworks' stock plummeting nearly 30 percent. To add fuel to the fire, CNN announced the same month that it would begin a free video service using Microsoft's Windows Media Player instead of the previously used Real technology.

Despite the stock setback, RealNetworks posted a quarterly profit in August 2005 on increased music subscriptions and reported earnings of $4.7 million, compared with a loss of $4.6 million the year prior. Revenue, meanwhile, rose to a record $82.7 million. CEO Glaser said his company would continue to concentrate on online music, games and other media as its core businesses and thus transform itself into a "consumer services company."

GETTING HIRED

Seattle's Best

RealNetworks lists detailed descriptions of openings on its web site, www.realnetworks.com/company/jobs, broken down by department. The jobs are surprisingly diverse, ranging from technical writing to managing advertising accounts, so the qualifications also vary. Some positions call for a degree in computer science; others demand an MBA. Experience in the computer industry is, of course, a plus. Many of the key managers at RealNetworks once worked for Microsoft, and the vice president of marketing was previously a congresswoman who represented a high tech district. Resumes can be submitted through an online form.

The company also runs an annual summer internship program for undergraduates, mainly in the fields of computer engineering, electrical engineering, mathematics, digital media, or those graduates on an MBA-track. All internships are located at company headquarters in Seattle and run for roughly 12 weeks. RealNetwork offers both competitive compensation and round-trip travel reimbursement for those outside of the Seattle area. RealNetworks posts a campus recruiting schedule on its career site as well.

Visit Vault at **www.vault.com** for insider company profiles, expert advice, career message boards, expert resume reviews, the Vault Job Board and more.

VAULT CAREER LIBRARY   **187**

OUR SURVEY SAYS

Work hard with bright minds

Without exception, employees say that working for RealNetworks means fairly flexible hours, a casual dress code and excellent opportunities for women and minorities. One employee, however said that "despite the company's flexibility, the hours number about 60 a week."

Despite formidable job descriptions on the company web site, the average employee age is young, including many recent grads and interns. Pay is competitive with other companies in the area. The company culture is described as exciting and energetic, and the employees as especially bright and independent. "We have people here working from all over the world," emphasizes one insider.

If you manage to land a job with RealNetworks, you'll have a leg up in the computer industry. "The company's name and reputation are so widely known that if you came here, you would be picked up faster than the same person who only worked at Microsoft," another insider explains.

Red Hat, Inc.

1801 Varsity Drive
Raleigh, NC 27606-2072
Phone: (919) 754-3700
Fax: (919) 754-3701
www.redhat.com

LOCATIONS

Raleigh, NC (HQ)
Huntsville, AL • Minneapolis, MN •
Mountain View, CA • Vienna, VA •
Westford, MA
More than 20 international
locations.

DEPARTMENTS

Applications and Tools Development •
Asia/Pacific Operations • Business
Development • Desktop Infrastructure
Technologies • Engineering •
Enterprise Group • Global Alliances •
Global Learning Services • Greater
China and North Asia • Human
Capital • Marketing • North American
Sales • Open Source Affairs •
Operating Systems Development •
Operations • Partner Development •
Product Management • Product
Strategy • Red Hat France and Italy •
Red Hat India • Red Hat Network •
Services • Worldwide Operations •
Worldwide Sales

THE STATS

Employer Type: Public Company
Stock Symbol: RHAT
Stock Exchange: NASDAQ
Chairman & CEO: Matthew J. (Matt)
Szulik
2005 Employees: 940
2005 Revenue ($mil.): $196.5

KEY COMPETITORS

Microsoft
Novell
SCO Group

EMPLOYMENT CONTACT

www.redhat.com/en_us/USA/home/
company/careers

Visit Vault at **www.vault.com** for insider company profiles, expert advice,
career message boards, expert resume reviews, the Vault Job Board and more.

VAULT CAREER LIBRARY   189

THE SCOOP

Hats off to Linux

Red Hat makes a living by causing the big guys to squirm: The company helped pioneer the use of Linux, the open source computer operating system that has become a chief rival to Microsoft's Windows systems. Red Hat—which also offers database, content, collaboration management applications; server and embedded operating systems; and software development tools—is relatively small potatoes compared to Microsoft, Novell and the like: fiscal year 2005 revenue topped only $196.5 million, although up from 2004.

That doesn't stop CEO Matthew Szulik from his self-described "bold mission" of implementing an aggressive strategy deemed "Open Source Architecture" (wooing corporate customers by blending Red Hat Enterprise Linux, Red Hat Network, Red Hat Applications and Services), "to become the defining technology company of the 21st century." With more than 160,000 Red Hat Enterprise Linux subscriptions sold during the 2004 fiscal year, and fiscal 2005 numbers that have shattered the year before, he does seem to have momentum on his side.

Finn-ishing school

Finnish grad student Linus Torvalds was the mastermind behind the Linux operating system, creating the programming code as a hobby in 1991, and then releasing it free over the Internet for anyone's use. A devoted following of programmers soon emerged, excited to find a no-cost alternative to the Microsoft Windows monopoly and eager to make their own revisions. Chief among them was IBM programmer, Marc Ewing, who began selling a new-and-improved version he'd developed called Red Hat (named after a cap his grandfather had given him.)

In 1994 Robert Young bought the rights to Ewing's creation and the two men formed Red Hat Software, Inc. The company began distributing Linux by CD-ROM and over the Internet (charging $50), but its main source of revenue was found in the manuals and technical support sold to new users and businesses challenged by the source code, which was constantly changing as improvements were made. In 1997 Red Hat and its Linux code still remained on the fringes of the high-tech world, mainly utilized by a select group of programmers who recognized and understood its possibilities.

Blowing up in the tech bubble ...

All this changed in 1998 when Intel and Netscape made small investments in the company, and Red Hat began making waves. The company announced it would form an enterprise computing division to bring Linux to businesses, and in 1999 Compaq, IBM, Novell, Oracle and SAP also invested in the company. In June of that year Red Hat went public with a huge IPO that catapulted 30-year-old Ewing to a seemingly lucky No. 13 on *Fortune* magazine's "40 Wealthiest Individuals Under 40" list.

Red Hat quickly used its newfound wealth to acquire Cygnus Solutions for $674 million and Hell's Kitchen Systems, maker of payment processing software. The company also underwent management changes, including Ewing's decision to retire, and President Matthew Szulik ascension to Young's position as CEO.

And then the bubble bursts

When the tech bubble burst in 2000, Red Hat went tumbling down with it, its stock plummeting a whopping 90 percent by 2001. But unlike many of its Internet counterparts, Red Hat actually did still have a viable product to offer, and the company worked on expanding into software products, including an e-commerce software suite designed for mid-sized businesses and database applications. In early 2002 there were rumors that AOL would purchase Red Hat, but nothing ever came of the speculation.

The company forged ahead as it developed these new technologies, increasing its revenue and stock price by 40 percent in 2002. By 2003 Red Hat was ready to resume its aggressive growth strategy, acquiring Sistina Software, which supplied data storage infrastructure software for Linux operating systems, for roughly $31 million in stock.

Big business

By the end of 2003 Red Hat had introduced a comprehensive Enterprise Linux version that sent profits soaring in fiscal year 2004, which ended in spring 2004. With a net income of $14 million, compared to a $6.6 million loss for fiscal year 2003, the company found itself once again in the black.

On a continued mission to encourage the corporate use of Linux, Red Hat ended routine maintenance on its Red Hat Linux line in 2004 (the company instead established the Fedora Project, a group of volunteer programmers who help with support issues for its original Linux distribution) so it could better focus on support

Visit Vault at **www.vault.com** for insider company profiles, expert advice, career message boards, expert resume reviews, the Vault Job Board and more.

V/\ULT CAREER LIBRARY   **191**

for its Red Hat Enterprise product. In early 2005 the company also established a government business unit and customers currently include the Department of Energy and the Federal Aviation Administration. Whereas technical support accounted for much of Red Hat's revenue in its early days, this segment is now less than one-third of the company's business as the Linux technology has become more mainstream and increasingly perfected; actual software subscriptions now account for around two-thirds of the company's revenue.

Nothing's free

One may be wondering: why would customers pay for subscriptions when they can still technically get the Linux code for free? In large part because Red Hat offers relatively inexpensive packages with customized software and tech support. But as Linux continues to gain in popularity (research firm IDC estimated that Linux accounted for 23.5 percent of the market for new server software shipments in 2002, second only to Microsoft's 55 percent, and ahead of Unix's 11 percent), competition from other companies offering Linux-based software also increases.

Powerhouse network software distributor Novell completely re-tooled its business model to embrace Linux (the move paid off with a $50 million investment from IBM, which has found integrating Linux with other computer services to be an increasingly lucrative business), and is currently Red Hat's chief competitor. Novell tends to focus on brand recognition, playing up its nearly 25 years of experience in the software development business. Red Hat, on the other hand, is most concerned with selling itself as the world leader and expert in Linux (many view the Red Hat name as being synonymous with Linux), always on the cutting edge and delivering a truer measure of open source to its customers. Judging by Red Hat's rapid growth, the strategy is paying off, although other Linux vendors are hardly the company's only competition.

Linux (rhymes with "cynics")

With the use of Linux rapidly on the rise, it was only a matter of time before sleeping-giant, Microsoft, was forced to take notice. Microsoft has always been notoriously tight-lipped about guarding the source codes for its operating system and desktop applications, but in 2001 it began cautiously allowing major clients to inspect the code, going so far as to give some the right to modify Window CE and even copyright modifications. In 2003 it began allowing many foreign governments to inspect Windows source code—many wanted assurance about security concerns (i.e. Microsoft wasn't allowing the CIA to infiltrate their information)—and it also became more aggressive in pursuing patents to protect its products. This patent portfolio has enabled Microsoft to bill itself as "standing behind" its products, a selling point meant to directly slam Linux providers, who found themselves embroiled in a murky copyrights lawsuit in 2003 that ultimately targeted their customers as well.

The issue was this: Linux had originally been developed to share some programming principles with Unix—an operating system developed by AT&T in the late 1960s and eventually licensed to some 6,000 universities, government agencies and businesses—so those who felt at home in a Unix environment could easily adapt. In 2001 Unix (and its licensing contracts) were acquired by SCO, and in 2003 SCO claimed that it had discovered fragments of Unix code in Linux. The company quickly sued IBM for allegedly dumping part of Unix into Linux, but also felt that additional fragments of non-IBM-placed Unix could be found in Linux, and began targeting companies that were Linux end users for violating its copyrights. In March 2004, it sued two Linux end users, AutoZone and DaimlerChrystler, scaring current and prospective Linux customers, who were worried that a few lines of code could force them to recall millions of devices.

You don't own me—or do you?

While Linux had already effectively accomplished what many thought was nearly impossible—curbing the Microsoft monopoly—the SCO situation is just one example of how foggy questions of legality and ownership present a multitude of possible headaches for customers and providers who rely on Linux—Red Hat chief among them. A May 2004 *Fortune* magazine article sums up this dilemma: "Linux is a morass of law-school exam questions waiting to be administered. In copyright terms, no one knows just what manner of beast it is. Is it a work of 'joint authorship'? A 'compilation'? A perpetually expanding service of 'derivative works'? Without knowing the answers to those questions, lawyers can't pinpoint precisely who owns either the whole of Linux or its fragments."

For now the Linux "beast" has meant continuing profits for Red Hat, which ended 2004 full steam ahead, despite a grim first half which saw stock plunge 30 percent, missed revenue projections and the surprise resignation of CFO Kevin Thompson for "family reasons." In September 2004 the company announced plans to acquire Netscape Enterprise Solutions from America Online, and Red Hat has actively sought entrance into lucrative overseas markets such as China, opening Red Hat Software (Beijing) Co. Ltd. in November 2004. Then, in May 2005, billionaire Michael S. Dell, founder and chairman of Dell Inc., infused Red Hat with $99.5 million through his private investment firm, MSD. The firm has also recently beefed up tools to help larger companies with multiple servers handle updates, fixes and other maintenance. And, though Red Hat sales slowed a bit during the summer of 2005, industry analysts foresee the open-source program market "evolving quickly to take on bigger jobs." If Szulik has his way, expect this to be just the beginning.

GETTING HIRED

Red around the world

Red Hat has grown to include approximately 940 employees in 27 offices worldwide. Job hunters should check out the careers section of its web site, www.redhat.com/about/careers, for information on recruiting events, benefits and job openings. Sign up for the job search agent and instantly receive e-mails about new openings that fit your criteria. Although there is a section for global openings, prospective employees can also find more information by accessing web sites for the individual countries in which Red Hat operates (links are included on the main site).

The site currently includes a diverse selection of internship opportunities, ranging from engineering to customer service, although most are located at the company's Raleigh, N.C., headquarters. Those interested can apply for these positions (as well as full-time openings) directly online. The careers section of the site also contains a number of first-person testimonials given by former and current Red Hat interns and employees, a good resource in evaluating what the company perceives to be its strengths and what it looks for in a prospective employee.

Top-notch benefits

Benefits include the opportunity to participate in medical, dental, vision and life insurance plans; a 401(k) retirement plan; employee stock purchase plan; tuition reimbursement plan; and an employee assistance program. An employee begins with 16 paid days off a year, nine paid holidays and three floating holidays. But the best benefit of working at Red Hat may be in convincing others to do the same: If a Red Hat employee refers a candidate who is then hired, he or she is eligible for a $2,000 bonus.

Sabre Holdings Corporation

3150 Sabre Drive
Southlake, TX 76092
Phone: (682) 605-1000
Fax: (682) 605-8267
www.sabre-holdings.com

LOCATIONS

Southlake, TX (HQ)
Operations in 45 countries.

Visit Vault at **www.vault.com** for insider company profiles, expert advice,
career message boards, expert resume reviews, the Vault Job Board and more.

VAULT CAREER LIBRARY   **195**

THE SCOOP

Reservation for No. 1

Sabre Holdings Company is a one-stop destination for travel, with the world's largest computerized global distribution system (Sabre Travel Network), the No. 1 travel reservations site (www.travelocity.com), and the leading provider of reservations systems and consulting services for airlines (Sabre Airline Solutions). The company also operates the brands GetThere, holidayautos, IgoUgo, lastminute.com, Nexion, Jurni Network, ShowTickets.com, Site 59, SynXis, Travelocity Business, and World Choice Travel. Travel reservations, not surprisingly, bring in nearly 70 percent of the company's overall revenue.

A meeting of like minds

The groundwork for Sabre was laid in 1953 after a chance meeting between C.R. Smith, then-president of American Airlines, and R. Blair Smith, a sales representative for IBM. In a discussion regarding the travel industry, the two men developed a plan for a data processing system that could create and manage airline seat reservations, then send such information to agents across the country. By the dawn of the 1960s, American Airlines and IBM jointly debuted the Semi-Automatic Business Research Environment—SABRE for short—in Briarcliff Manor, N.Y., with a mainframe that processed 84,000 telephone calls daily. Within four years, the data processing system had become the nation's second-largest private system, trailing only the U.S. government.

The SABRE system hit travel agencies in 1976, and had recorded over one million fares by 1978. The program was further improved during the 1980s, eventually reaching personal computers in 1985. AMR, American Airlines' parent company, purchased Sabre the following year, while the SABRE system debuted in the European travel market. In 1988, Sabre Airline Solutions began providing software, consulting and systems management services to other airlines, and eclipsed storage capabilities of 36 million fares. A flight rescheduling system, RESARAIL system for rail reservations in Europe, and a joint venture with ABACUS International to establish the SabreSonic passenger solution in Asia were among the innovation highlights during the 1990s.

Travel abroad

To kick off the new millennium, Sabre completely spun off from AMR in 2000, the same year it purchased GetThere, an online corporate travel booking tool. In 2001, Sabre acquired the Sabre Pacific travel distribution business from TIAS, a travel alliance between Qantas, Air New Zealand and Ansett Airlines, thus expanding the firm's presence in the South Pacific region.

International expansion was on the company's mind again in 2002, as Sabre picked up the shares of Travelocity it didn't already own in a hostile takeover worth $345 million. The purchase added Travelocity Europe, a multi-channel travel company and also one of the leading European direct travel agencies, and Site59 an online purveyor of last-minute model air, hotel and rental car inventory, to the Sabre fold. Meanwhile, Travelocity brought in $359 million in revenue and $3.9 billion in gross bookings and accounted for 14 percent of Sabre's revenue in 2002.

Down but not out

In November 2002, the firm announced plans to cut 5 to 7 percent of its workforce to reduce costs as the travel and tourism industry attempted to regain footing following the September 11 terrorist attacks. By the end of 2002, the firm had cut its fourth-quarter and full-year earnings forecasts. Sabre remained "cautious" into 2003 with regards to hiring, and announced plans to let go of more than 500 workers in that October, its fourth round of layoffs in as many years. Sabre also closed its Travelocity headquarters in Fort Worth, and dissolved GetThere, its corporate travel technology unit, into three other units. On the customer service end, the firm released Travelocity Business to serve corporate travel agencies and business travelers, and TotalTrip, offering new packaging capabilities, and began offering air travel insurance to customers. Sabre also acquired World Choice Travel, a hotel room consolidation and distribution business.

Spinning a world wide web

At the start of 2005, Sabre joined with Middle East carrier Gulf Air to create Sabre Travel Network Middle East, a joint venture based in Bahrain, in an effort to push the company into Middle Eastern markets. Meanwhile, Travelocity launched its French consumer travel web site, Odysia. On the Web, Sabre picked up IgoUgo.com, a travel community web site, and lastminute.com, Europe's leading online travel site, with roughly 2,000 employees, and also launched the industry's first travel keyword search engine.

Visit Vault at **www.vault.com** for insider company profiles, expert advice, career message boards, expert resume reviews, the Vault Job Board and more.

VAULT CAREER LIBRARY   197

GETTING HIRED

Sabre service

The career section of Sabre's web site, www.sabre-holdings.com/careers/index.html, divides jobs by location (U.S. and abroad), and allows job seekers to create a profile and upload a resume (recruiters routinely scan the profile database for candidates). In addition, the company runs a summer internship program for students with placements in the fields of finance, marketing and technology, and currently recruits at Cornell University, Florida Institute of Technology, Indiana University, Massachusetts Institute of Technology, Southern Methodist University, Texas A&M University, Texas Christian University, the University of North Texas and the University of Texas at Arlington, Austin and Dallas.

OUR SURVEY SAYS

Friendly and casual

Sabre provides its "hardworking and friendly" employees with the "latest in technology." The company has established a relaxed dress code—most employees wear business casual or even jeans—and workers feel that the policy is indicative of a "congenial" and "laid-back" atmosphere. One longtime company employee says that he feels the office offers an "unusually receptive" environment for minorities, lesbians and gays. Even though Sabre has split off from American Airlines, employees still enjoy unlimited, "substantial" air travel discounts that enables them to "travel every weekend." The spin-off from American, meanwhile, has caused very little disruption at Sabre. Employees are enthusiastic about the change and believe that "now the company can reach its potential."

Salon Media Group, Inc.

1 Rincon Center
101 Spear Street, Suite 203
San Francisco, CA 94105
Phone: (415) 645-9200
Fax: (415) 645-9204
www.salon.com

LOCATIONS

San Francisco, CA (HQ)
New York, NY
Washington, DC

THE STATS

Employer Type: Public Company
Stock Symbol: SALN
Stock Exchange: OTC
Chairman: David Talbot
CEO: Elizabeth Hambrecht
2004 Employees: 55
2004 Revenue ($mil.): $4.5

KEY COMPETITORS

CNN
New York Times Digital
Slate Magazine

EMPLOYMENT CONTACT

www.salon.com/about/hiring/index.
 html

THE SCOOP

Does quality count?

Is there a place for quality content on the Web? Pioneering online magazine purveyor Salon Media Group (formerly Salon.com) sure thinks so. Its publication, which features breaking news as well as top-notch authors like Camille Paglia, Arianna Huffington and Garrison Keillor in addition to a host of other columnists and reviewers, is one of the few Web-only serious news sources. Part of that effort has included the acquisition of San Francisco-based The Well, one of the oldest Internet communities.

Salon produces a network of 11 award-winning, original content sites that provide news, features, interviews, blogs and regular columnists on specific topics ranging from arts and entertainment to politics, parenting and health. It also hosts MP3Lit.com, a digital audio literature site, as well as two online communities—Table Talk and The Well, which have more than 80,000 subscribers. Salon has won most major web awards including three straight Webby's, "Best Website" by *Entertainment Weekly*, "Best of the Web" by *BusinessWeek* and "Website of the Year" by *Time* magazine.

Turning content into cash

Because it is very difficult to get web users to pay for content, Salon monetizes its content in other ways. The company's revenue is drawn heavily from online advertising as well as content licensing and subscription fees. Salon broadened its reach (and name recognition) through a number of distribution deals in 1999 and early 2000, and strategic distribution agreements with Lycos, AltaVista, Reuters, CNN.com and CNET, as well as content licensing. Salon also aligned itself with SpeakOut.com, whose online activism tools enhanced Salon.com's News and Politics2000 sites, as well as the online community area Table Talk.

In 2000 Salon announced an agreement with Bravo Networks to produce a television show intended to be a cross between *60 Minutes* and *Monty Python*. It would reflect Salon's web site, covering news, interviews and cultural issues. In May 2000, Salon also announced the acquisition of MP3Lit.com, the first web site dedicated to offering spoken word and audio literature recordings in the MP3 format. Under the terms of the agreement, Salon put up $5 million worth of stocks and cash in exchange for all outstanding shares of MP3Lit.com.

One day at a time

In an effort to attract more readers and allow for more advertising, Salon relaunched its web site in spring 2000. The fifth version in five years generated heated outcry from many readers. The company responded with a partial retread, keeping much of the redesign but changing the home page in response to users preferences.

However, Salon faced more ominous problems. The company announced in June 2000 that due to the $14 million in expected revenue and $28 million in expected expenses, Salon cut its operating budget by 20 percent and laid off 10 percent of its staff. Then-CEO Michael O'Donnell's explained the restructuring as crucial to the site's survival: "You need to make sure that you'll live another day."

Survival

Though Salon completed its June 1999 public offering with shares closing at $10, by July 2000 the stock was on the verge of getting booted off Nasdaq, with share price hovering just above $1. A year later, Salon laid off another 14 employees and converted its message boards to a paid service to cut costs and boost revenue. Meanwhile, Bill Hambrecht, chairman and CEO of W.R. Hambrecht and Co., kicked in a much needed $2.5 million in financing for the struggling company. Despite the boost, Salon lost $6.6 million during the first nine months of its 2001 fiscal year, prompting an additional $500,000 infusion of cash from software maker Adobe Systems in March 2002.

A new blogging service, which debuted in July 2002, offered subscribers the chance to build and maintain their own personal online journals at a cost of $39.95 a year, part of a plan to generate revenue. By February 2003, though, Salon announced it would be unable to continue operations without additional financing. Hambrecht and John Warnock, founder of Adobe, kicked in $800,000 in the nick of time, in hopes that the company would be able to become self-sufficient. CEO Michael O'Donnell bowed out that October after seven years with the company, replaced by founder, chairman and editor-in-chief David Talbot.

Like a rolling stone

At the start of 2004, Salon announced a partnership with Jann Wenner, chairman of Wenner media, through which Salon and Wenner's *Rolling Stone* would collaborate on a series of articles regarding the 2004 presidential election. In addition, Wenner invested $200,000 in Salon, and joined the firm's board. Talbot said the Wenner venture was part of a larger plan to boost Salon's political coverage—which also

Visit Vault at www.vault.com for insider company profiles, expert advice, career message boards, expert resume reviews, the Vault Job Board and more.

VAULT CAREER LIBRARY   201

included hiring Sidney Blumenthal, former aide to President Clinton, as consultant and columnist. The power of politics proved strong: by the second-quarter reported September 2004, subscribers were up by more than 8,000 and a 2003 net loss of $1.2 million had turned into a net gain of $1 million.

Management on a mission

Salon started 2005 off with some major management changes. Elizabeth Hambrecht joined as CEO, Joan Walsh signed on as editor-in-chief, and Conrad Lowry became the chief financial officer, while Talbot remained chairman of the board. Walsh joined the company in 1998, and oversaw the development of the news and politics department; Hambrecht, the daughter of investor Bill Hambrecht, had previously been Salon's CFO and president. The company's loss margin narrowed to $607,000 in the fourth quarter of 2004, compared with a loss of $5 million the year prior, while advertising sales were up to $700,000 from $400,000.

A complete turnaround was momentarily put on hold by the summer of 2005, which saw a loss of $116,000. CEO Hambrecht admitted she was "disappointed" by the results in the first quarter, which included a drop in ad sales. Salon also expected to lose money in the second quarter.

GETTING HIRED

Don't call us, we'll call you

Job openings are posted at salon.com/about/hiring/index.html. Resumes can be sent by e-mail or postal mail, but the company will not respond to phone inquiries.

Shopping.com

8000 Marina Boulevard, Fifth Floor
Brisbane, CA 94005
Phone: (650) 616-6500
Fax: (650) 616-6510
www.shopping.com

LOCATIONS

Brisbane, CA (HQ)
London
Netanva, Israel

THE STATS

Employer Type: Subsidiary of eBay Inc.
CEO: Lorrie M. Norrington
2004 Employees: 310
2004 Revenue ($mil.): $99

KEY COMPETITORS

mySimon
Shopzilla
Yahoo!

EMPLOYMENT CONTACT

www.shopping.com/aa16-jobs

Visit Vault at **www.vault.com** for insider company profiles, expert advice, career message boards, expert resume reviews, the Vault Job Board and more.

VAULT CAREER LIBRARY   203

THE SCOOP

Let's make a deal

Founded by two Israeli high-tech entrepreneurs in December 1997, Shopping.com, formerly DealTime.com, went live with its online shopping comparison service in June 1999, backed by venture capital funding from firms like Israel Seed Partners and Odeon Capital Partners, as well as by strategic and financial partners including AOL, Time Warner and Bank of America. The site uses an automated shopping "bot" to comb hundreds of web sites—including online merchants, auctions, classifieds and group buying sites—to find the lowest prices on thousands of items. DealTime also allows consumers to compare prices with offline sellers. Shopping.com now ranks as the leading comparison-shopping engine on the Web, earning revenue from referral fees. The site, which lists the prices for over two million retail items from thousands of online merchants, was picked up by online auction firm eBay for $620 million in June 2005.

A wide range of products and services

Price-conscious shoppers can browse DealTime's categories, which include pet supplies, electronics, health and beauty, and video games, and then search by brand name, product model or keyword within each category. Once a search is completed, consumers have the option of sorting results by merchant, merchant rating (from bizrate.com), product, deal type or price. DealTime then provides a link to each merchant's web site. A partnership with epinions.com spawned dealtime.epinions.com, which provides access to reviews of consumer products. Other features of DealTime's main site include the Desktop Notifier, a software download that provides price updates; e-mail or pager notifications of lower prices; and DealAgent, a service for merchants that tracks shoppers' click-throughs and price requests in each category, and allows merchants to respond immediately by submitting a new price on the site.

The high-stakes battle for the top

As a number of new shopping comparison sites mounted a direct challenge to DealTime's service, the company launched a $25 million advertising campaign in the fall 1999 intended to raise the company's profile prior to the crucial holiday shopping period. In February 2000, the company announced that it had raised $50 million in private placement. In April 2003, DealTime merged with consumer review site

Epinions.com and in September 2003, the combined company relaunched as Shopping.com. Greg Santora, a former CFO and senior vice president at Intuit, Inc., came aboard as CFO of the new site. At the same time, Nirav Tolia, the founder of epinions.com, resigned as COO of the company and from the board of directors after management became aware of inaccuracies in Tolia's resume.

Sold!

Shopping.com had a successful IPO in October 2004 that saw its shares rise more than 50 percent in the first day of trading. Stock soared 60 percent at the outset to a high of $28.80 after debuting at $18, though analysts warned the rally might not last. In fact, Shopping.com reported a loss of $5.5 million for the fiscal year ended that December, compared with a net income of $6.9 million the year prior. Despite the slip, revenue increased from $67 million in 2003 to $99 million in 2004.

In April 2005, Lorrie Norrington, a member of the board of directors, became Shopping.com's CEO, replacing Dan Ciporin. Norrington was previously an executive vice president at Intuit. Ciporin praised his replacement for her "track record of growing and scaling global enterprises." Revenue and unique visitors continued to climb during the spring of 2005, garnering the attention of another Internet shopping mecca: eBay. The online auctioneer bought Shopping.com in June 2005 for $620 million in cash as part of a strategic plan to increase site traffic.

GETTING HIRED

Shopping for a career

Shopping.com posts job opportunities on its career web site, www.shopping.com/aa16-jobs. All positions are located in the San Francisco area. Resumes should be e-mailed to jobs@shopping.com, with the job you are applying for listed in the subject header.

Visit Vault at **www.vault.com** for insider company profiles, expert advice, career message boards, expert resume reviews, the Vault Job Board and more.

V/\ULT CAREER LIBRARY   **205**

Sportsline.com, Inc.

2200 W. Cypress Creek Road
Fort Lauderdale, FL 33309
Phone: (954) 489-4000
Fax: (954) 771-2807
www.cbs.sportsline.com

LOCATION

Fort Lauderdale, FL (HQ)

THE STATS

Employer Type: Subsidiary of CBS
President, CBS Digital: Larry Kramer
2004 Employees: 247
2003 Revenue ($mil.): $57.7

KEY COMPETITORS

Fox Sports
Disney Internet
Yahoo!

EMPLOYMENT CONTACT

SportsLine.com, Inc.
Attn: Employment
2200 W. Cypress Creek Road
Fort Lauderdale, FL 33309
Fax: (954) 252-4039
E-mail: dmemployment@cbs.com

THE SCOOP

Always room for more

When Michael Levy founded SportsLine USA in 1994, many analysts believed that the media was already super-saturated with sports information, and that another venue was unnecessary. The online service, since renamed SportsLine.com, has overcome its critics; today, it is one of the leading sports sites, providing sports-related information and entertainment to more than 7 million users. The flagship site features scores, statistics, streaming audio and video, fantasy leagues, news and commentary and covers the four major professional sports in the U.S. (baseball, basketball, football and hockey) as well as college sports, golf, tennis and auto racing. Visitors to the Sportsline.com can partake in free fantasy games, noted by *Forbes* magazine as among the best. In the 2005 *Forbes* Web Site Reviews, SportsLine also earned notice for MySportsLine, which allows subscribers to track their favorite sports, teams and players, and for the best NCAA basketball coverage. In addition to its eponymous web site, SportsLine also publishes the official web sites of the NFL, PGA Tour and NCAA.

Let's make a deal

Back in 1997, when SportsLine wasn't the household name it is today, the company struck a deal with CBS: In return for a branding campaign which broadcast CBS SportsLine on millions of television screens each week, SportsLine agreed to pay CBS $60 million in stock. In 2003, the company's first $20 million payment behind it, SportsLine CEO Mike Levy commented that it didn't seem like such a bad deal when the stock was at $40, but at $2 per share, it seemed likely that CBS would eventually gain full ownership.

In December 2004, Levy's prediction became a reality. Viacom (which merged with CBS in 1999) completed its acquisition of the remaining stake in SportsLine.com. The parent company paid $46 million for the additional 62 percent. Initially, SportsLine operated as a division of CBS Sports, reporting to Sean McManus, President of CBS Sports. In March 2005, however, Viacom created a new division, CBS Digital, including CBS.com, CBS Sportsline.com, CBSNews.com and UPN.com, which is headed up by Larry Kramer.

Visit Vault at **www.vault.com** for insider company profiles, expert advice, career message boards, expert resume reviews, the Vault Job Board and more.

VAULT CAREER LIBRARY   207

GETTING HIRED

Fill out an application

SportsLine.com advises interested individuals to search for current openings through hotjobs.com. Simply type in "SportsLine" in the "Quick Job Search Keywords" box. Candidates can also send resumes directly to the company, but online applications will receive the quickest review.

Spring Street Networks

419 Lafayette Street
New York, NY 10003
Phone: (212) 929-8890
Fax: (212) 929-9046
www.springstreetnetworks.com

LOCATION

New York, NY (HQ)

THE STATS

Employer Type: Subsidiary of Various, Inc.
CEO: Louis Kanganis

KEY COMPETITORS

Friendster
Lavalife
Match.com

EMPLOYMENT CONTACT

www.springstreetnetworks.com/careers

Visit Vault at **www.vault.com** for insider company profiles, expert advice, career message boards, expert resume reviews, the Vault Job Board and more.

V∧ULT CAREER LIBRARY   209

THE SCOOP

Word on the street

Spring Street Networks wants to help you find your soulmate. Since 2002, the company has maintained a growing database of personal profiles—2 million as of August 2005—and partnered with some 200 media companies, including *The Onion*, Village Voice Media, Salon Media, Nerve.com and Primedia/New York Media, to spread its personal ads from coast to coast. The company generates revenue by charging users to contact each other, then splits the profit with the content provider, and bills itself as "the only personals company whose mission is to be the best partner for content brands."

Getting personal

Online personals are among the most profitable and fast-growing Internet businesses. At the time Spring Street was conceived, consumers spent more than $300 million on online personal ads, according to 2002 data culled from the Online Publishers Association. In July 2003, Spring Street picked up $6 million in funding from Battery Ventures, a venture capital firm focused on technology investments, to support product development and market initiatives, on the strength of the bustling personals business.

The firm quickly became a leading provider of private-label online personal solutions through a strategic platform of allowing partners to create the look of their site on the front-end, while leveraging data to partners behind the scenes, thus allowing subscribers from one partner to interact with those of another. In July 2005, Spring Street was acquired by San Francisco-based Various Inc., parent company of FriendFinder, the world's largest operator of dating and social networking web sites, for an undisclosed amount. Spring Street will maintain its SoHo headquarters in New York City, and looks to increase its staff in the months following the close of the deal.

GETTING HIRED

Perks and quirks

Spring Street lists job availabilities on its career site, www.springstreetnetworks.com/careers. The company lists job descriptions and contact information, as well as the lowdown on all aspects of working at Spring Street, including both the "cool" (such as helping with marketing campaigns, for example) and "not as exciting" (post office runs, anyone?).

Visit Vault at **www.vault.com** for insider company profiles, expert advice, career message boards, expert resume reviews, the Vault Job Board and more.

V/\ULT CAREER LIBRARY   **211**

Sterling Commerce, Inc.

4600 Lakehurst Court
Dublin, OH 43016-2000
Phone: (614) 793-7000
Fax: (614) 793-4040
www.sterlingcommerce.com

LOCATIONS

Dublin, OH (HQ)
Ann Arbor, MI
Atlanta, GA
Boston, MA
Chicago, IL
Dallas, TX
Los Angeles, CA
New York, NY
Parsippany, NJ
San Francisco, CA
Washington, DC
Additional offices worldwide.

DEPARTMENTS

Business Applications
Business Integration
Business Intelligence
Business Process Management
Supply Chain Management

THE STATS

Employer Type: Subsidiary of AT&T
President and CEO: Samuel Starr
2004 Employees: 1600+
2004 Revenue ($mil.): $460.9

KEY COMPETITORS

GXS
IBM
webMethods

EMPLOYMENT CONTACT

www.sterlingcommerce.com/About/
  Careers

THE SCOOP

Working for the big boys

Sterling Commerce provides business-to-business commerce solutions for some 29,000 companies, including 73 percent of the Fortune 100 and 76 percent of the Forbes European 100. Four out of five Fortune 500 companies rely on Sterling Commerce to improve their business processes—and profitability. The company's client list reads like a who's who of business moguls; Chrysler, Heinz, Home Depot, Honeywell, Williams Sonoma and Wachovia are just few. Sterling Commerce focuses on the banking, health care, industrial manufacturing, logistics and retail sectors, providing solutions in the areas of business integration, business intelligence, business process management, business applications and supply chain management.

Changing with the times

Sterling Commerce has been in the B2B biz for 30 years and is recognized as a pioneer of electronic data interchange (EDI) and secure file transfer technology. Formerly a division of Sterling Software, Sterling Commerce was spun off in March 1996 and quickly grew to become one of the world's largest independent providers of multi-enterprise collaborative solutions. In March 2000, the company was snatched up by SBC Communications. At that time, the company boasted some 2,500 employees, more than 50,000 clients and around $550 million in revenue.

The B2B landscape has changed significantly since Internet boom times. The industry shrank from around 1,500 independent businesses in 2001 to roughly 200 by the end of 2003. But, Sterling Commerce continues to innovate and remain a leader. In fact, within the last year, Sterling Commerce was the only integration vendor to achieve Leader status in all three of Gartner Group's Magic Quadrants in that space: It was Leader in Integration as a Service November 2004, Leader in B2B Gateway in April 2005, and Leader in Integration Backbone also in April 2005.

Forrester Research also cited Sterling Commerce as a leader in integration suites in terms of executive vision, installed base, financial viability and solution cost. The July 2005 report lauds Sterling for moving beyond its roots and "developing a fully functional integration suite that addresses the combined enterprise application integration (EAI), B2B integration (B2Bi) and business process management (BPM) capability." Forrester also described Sterling as "one of the most aggressive in

Visit Vault at **www.vault.com** for insider company profiles, expert advice, career message boards, expert resume reviews, the Vault Job Board and more.

VAULT CAREER LIBRARY   213

pursuing advanced integration capability during the past three years—and the results are impressive."

The new numbers

Although Sterling's numbers have decreased somewhat since boom times, the company is still plugging along, adapting its offerings to meet the changing B2B environment. Sterling now employs a staff of more than 2,000 working out of offices all over the globe. For 2004, the company posted revenues of $461 million and a net loss of $573,000.

GETTING HIRED

A Sterling experience

Candidates interested in working for Sterling Commerce can check out current job openings online. College students looking to get their foot in the door—or just an interesting experience—should check into Sterling's internship and co-op opportunities, listed under "College Connection." Sterling offers a comprehensive benefits package, including 401(k) matching, health insurance, vacation and sick leave, tuition reimbursement, floating holidays, free life insurance and adoption assistance.

Terra Networks, S.A.

95 Merrick Way, Suite 706
Coral Gables, FL 33134
Phone: (786) 552-1400
www.terra.com

LOCATION

Coral Gables, FL (HQ)
Seattle, WA • Puerto Rico •
Argentina • Brazil • Chile •
Columbia • Costa Rica • Dominican
Republic • El Salvador • Guatemala •
Hondorus • Mexico • Nicaragua •
Panama • Peru • Uruguay •
Venezuela

DEPARTMENT

Sales

Visit Vault at **www.vault.com** for insider company profiles, expert advice,
career message boards, expert resume reviews, the Vault Job Board and more.

VAULT CAREER LIBRARY   215

THE SCOOP

Crossing cultures

Michael Mauldin, a former researcher at the Center for Machine Translation at Carnegie Mellon University, is the technological genius who created what was then known as the Lycos search engine. Microsoft and the Library Corporation licensed the technology in 1995, a year after Mauldin left the center. CMG@Ventures soon purchased the company, which was named Lycos, Inc., and Robert Davis was named president and CEO. In 1996, the company went public with an initial public offering of $177 million; however, Barcelona-based Terra Networks soon hit the scene. An eminent ISP among Spanish and Portuguese-speaking markets, Terra Networks soon acquired the Waltham, Mass.-based Lycos, combining local and global content with web search engines and services. In October 2000, Terra Networks, S.A. purchased Lycos in a stock deal worth $12.5 billion. With a strategy of reaching the Hispanic market, Terra Lycos now had access to more than 30 million Spanish speakers in the U.S. Bertelsmann AG, one of the world's largest media companies, was also a part of the alliance. The German corporation agreed to purchase $1 billion worth of advertising, placement and integration services from Terra Lycos, expanding upon the mega-company's already existing relationship with Lycos Europe

A smorgasbord of services

To keep web surfers coming back, Lycos employed a number of creative strategies to lure them in. These strategies became even more creative after the Terra Networks/Lycos pairing. The company strongly believes that focusing on a group of communities that will keep users engaged, rather than letting them wander off to another destination, is what gives them a competitive edge. For example, surfers can log on to a number of different web sites, all part of the large Terra Lycos umbrella, and feel at ease within an online community that's targeted to their exact needs. In addition to TerraLycos.com and Lycos.com, the communities include AnimationExpress.com, displaying the best animations on the Web; Angelfire.com and Tripod.com, where users create and self-publish homepages; ATuHora.com, a one-hour delivery service; Gamesville.com, a multiplayer, real-time game site, where members compete for prizes by playing each other; search engine hotbot.com; financial sites Invertia.com, RagingBull.com and Quote.com; Matchmaker.com, an online dating resource; LycosZone, for children; travel portal Rumbo.com;

Sonique.com, an audioplayer; WhoWhere.com, an online guide to the white and yellow pages; and Wired.com, the online version of *Wired* magazine.

Good sports

One marketing ploy for Terra Lycos included signing up to endorse tennis star Anna Kournikova, teaming up with American Media, publishers of the *Star* and other gossip publications, to feature content on the Lycos Entertainment channel. The company also incorporated eBay item listings and categories into the Lycos Auctions destination. The Tripod.com web site introduced its Tripod Blog Builder in 2003 in the hopes of luring in subscribers. Here, surfers can see their daily musings posted online immediately. Terra Lycos charges $4.95-$19.95 a month for these services. In 2002, FOXSports joined Terra Lycos to create cutting-edge content for sports enthusiasts. On Lycos.com, FOXSports.com's broadcast and television promotions are broadcast. In return, FOX TV, including FOX World, FOX Sports Net and FOX Sports, promotes Lycos. Foxsports.lycos.com, a web site available globally, gives both companies the chance to sell joint advertising packages.

Staying afloat

Terra Lycos is headed by Executive Chairman Joaquin Agut. Once of General Electric, the former Terra Networks chairman replaced Robert Davis. The company continues to maintain a model of open, basic and premium services. This way, users can log on for free and surf without any commitment. If they like what they see or want to explore content that is available only to paying customers, they can upgrade. There are 31 million paying subscribers, comprising 48 percent of Terra Lycos users.

Terra Lycos posted a record loss of 2.01 billion Euros in 2003, which company officials feel is due in part to a loss of ad contract with Bertelsmann AG. But that's not the only bad news. Revenue plummeted to 114.8 million Euros from 160.6 million Euros. To cut costs, U.S. employees were reduced by 22 percent. The company also sold its stake in the Lycos Japan portal. As of 2003 Terra Lycos boasted 3,000 advertisers, 4.35 million subscribers and 500 million daily page views. Also in 2003, Telefonica SA implemented a 1 billion Euro takeover of Terra Lycos, settling for 72 percent of the company. Telefonica remains the company's main shareholder and biggest client

Terra Networks is a leading Internet services and online content provider targeting Spanish-speaking customers in Spain and Latin America. The company agreed to be bought out by parent Telefonica, Spain's leading telecommunications operator, in

Visit Vault at **www.vault.com** for insider company profiles, expert advice, career message boards, expert resume reviews, the Vault Job Board and more.

VAULT CAREER LIBRARY   **217**

February 2005. Terra stopped trading on July 15 and is now a wholly owned subsidiary of Telefonica. Terra shareholders received two Telefonica shares for every nine Terra shares.

Terra is tops

Despite the dot-com slump, Terra is now one of the world's leading Internet service providers (ISPs) Terra Lycos reaches out to 118 million users a month in 43 countries and 19 different languages with a slew of innovative Internet services. It offers dial-up and broadband Internet service to nearly 2 million subscribers primarily in Spain, Brazil and Chile. It also operates portal web sites serving audiences in about 30 countries and generates revenue primarily through advertising, offering news and entertainment content as well as e-commerce and communications services.

GETTING HIRED

Spanish speakers need apply

Terra Networks' web site is written mostly in Spanish, so job seekers should be fluent in the language or at least have a working knowledge of it. There is a career section www.terra.com/trabaja. Though most of the rest of the site is in Spanish, the jobs available section is provided in English. Applicants can also send resumes in by snail mail to: Terra Networks Operations, Inc., 95 Merrick Way, Suite 706, Coral Gables, Florida 33134, Attn.: Director of Operations Recruitment.

theglobe.com, Inc.

110 E. Broward Blvd., Ste. 1400
Fort Lauderdale, FL 33301
Phone: (954) 769-5900
Fax: (954) 769-5930
www.voiceglo.com

LOCATION

Fort Lauderdale, FL (HQ)

THE STATS

Employer Type: Public Company
Stock Symbol: TGLO
Stock Exchange: OTC
Chairman & CEO: Michael S. Egan
2004 Employees: 118
2004 Revenue ($mil.): $16.0

KEY COMPETITORS

CNET Networks
Future Network USA
Skype

EMPLOYMENT CONTACT

www.voiceglo.com

Visit Vault at **www.vault.com** for insider company profiles, expert advice,
career message boards, expert resume reviews, the Vault Job Board and more.

VAULT CAREER LIBRARY   219

THE SCOOP

No beer, just Web

Not all college kids sit around and drink beer. Some, like entrepreneurs Todd Krizelman and Stephan Paternot, start multimillion-dollar companies. theglobe.com, a comprehensive community web site, started at Cornell University, but ended in an amazing IPO and a success story for the 1990s. The two coeds started theglobe.com in their dorm room in 1995. By 1996 the company had 17 employees (average age: 22); Krizelman and Paternot assuaged the pain of long hours with free pizza. The duo conceived of theglobe.com as a sort of universal web site.

After registering through a detailed questionnaire, theglobe.com members have access to a potpourri of free services, including free e-mail, space to build web pages, access to bulletin boards and chat services to mingle (virtually) with other theglobe.com members, and specially tailored promotions. In fact, the Cornell students had managed to construct one of the first viable web communities, along with Geocities and America Online.

A car full of dollars

The company truly took off when Krizelman and Paternot were introduced to Michael Egan, co-founder of Alamo Rent-a-car. Egan, impressed by the two young entrepreneurs, invested a cool $20 million into theglobe.com. With the massive cash infusion, Wall Street took a good long look at the burgeoning community.

theglobe.com scheduled an IPO in September 1998, but a sudden slide in Internet stocks caused Bear Stearns, theglobe.com's issuer, to mothball the IPO. Two months later, Bear Stearns yanked theglobe.com back on the market in November 1998. Incredibly, after pricing at $9, theglobe.com went on to hit a high of $97 dollars a share that day—a rise of over 600 percent, one of the top IPO debuts in history.

Evaluating the moon (or globe) shot

Since that high point, theglobe.com stock dropped precipitously. Despite its millions of members and revenue of $5.5 million in 1998, the company, like most Internet darlings, continued to lose money into the late 1990s, and forced the ousting of co-CEO's Paternot and Krizelman at the start of 2000. Charles Peck stepped up to the plate as CEO that August. Peck had 30 years of sales and marketing experience, including a stint as vice president at the American Institute of Certified Public Accountants.

Creating community

Although theglobe.com was named as one of the "Top of the Net: 100 Best Sites for 2000" in the category of "Best Free Web Pages" in the January 2000 issue of *Yahoo! Internet Life*, as well as the most trafficked site on the Web in the "Community" category by *Media Metrix* in March 2000, theglobe.com still had a ways to go. In an effort to turn a profit, the firm began business-to-business deals by providing software and services to other sites like CBS SportsLine, Deja.com and RollingStone.com. A partnership with e-Net, Inc. provided theglobe.com with ZeroPlus.com's telephony services, including free Internet telephony services and other fee-based features. theglobe.com also drafted a strategic plan to provide "community" through four streams: its web site with e-mail clubs and forums; the second, customized community solutions to other web properties; small business communities; and games.theglobe.com, a games information network offering the Happy Puppy, Kids Domain and Web Jump game sites among others.

Ch-ch-ch-changes

A year later, most of theglobe's original offerings—including chat rooms and free e-mail accounts—had been cancelled as the company struggled to stay afloat in the slumping Internet market. Peck built a business plan focused on the firm's gaming information unit, building up theglobe's online game property site. That plan soon proved futile as well, and, in August 2001, Peck announced plans to cut 60 jobs, nearly half the company's workforce, shut down the firm's business web site (www.theglobe.com) and its small-business web-hosting site (www.webjump.com).

By 2004, the company was a ghost of its former self, launching its hope for the future on the back of Voiceglo, a VoIP service, and on the purchase of SendTec, a direct response marketing services subsidiary. These days, profit comes mostly from SendTec services, as well as from the firm's games division, which derives revenue from sales of *Computer Games* magazine, video games through the firm's Chips & Bits business, and online ads. And, as the VoIP market grows stronger, theglobe is hoping its Voiceglo service will eventually be a major competitor to traditional phone services like Verizon and the Bells.

GETTING HIRED

No info

There is no hiring information on the company's web site. Interested applicants can send a query to Michele M. Merrell at mmerrell@voiceglo.com.

Travelocity.com LP

3150 Sabre Drive
Southlake, TX 76092
Phone: (682) 605-3000
Fax: (817) 785-8004
www.travelocity.com

LOCATIONS

Southlake, TX (HQ)
New York, NY
North Palm Beach, FL
Plains, PA
San Antonio, TX
San Francisco, CA
Sydney

DEPARTMENTS

Cars
Cruises
Customer Care
Destination Guides
Flights
Hotels
Last Minute Deals

THE STATS

Employer Type: Subsidiary of Sabre
President and CEO: Michelle Peluso
2004 Revenue ($mil.): $502.5

KEY COMPETITORS

Expedia
Orbitz
Priceline

EMPLOYMENT CONTACT

www.sabre-holdings.com/careers/
    index.html (enter keyword:
    Travelocity)

Visit Vault at **www.vault.com** for insider company profiles, expert advice,
career message boards, expert resume reviews, the Vault Job Board and more.

VAULT CAREER LIBRARY   223

THE SCOOP

Thrifty travel

The No. 2 online travel agency, Travelocity is a one-stop shop for budget-conscious consumers in search of plane tickets, hotel rooms, car rentals, cruises and vacation packages. Best known for its eponymous web site, Travelocity also operates a number of other sites (in 12 different languages), most notably holidayautos.com, lastminute.com, Showtickets.com, Site59, Travelocity Business and World Choice Travel.

Launched in 1996 as a joint venture of Worldview Systems Corp., publisher of online destination information, and Sabre Interactive (now Sabre Holdings), Travelocity gained limited freedom in March 2000 when it staged a partial initial public offering. Two years later, in April 2002, Sabre reined the online travel company back in, buying up the 30 percent of Travelocity it had spun-off. Today, Travelocity is a wholly owned subsidiary of Sabre Holdings, contributing 22 percent of sales in 2004.

Turbulent times

In the past few years, Travelocity has seen its fair share of turbulence. The former bright star and market share leader in the online travel biz slipped to the number two position in 2002 and has been playing catch-up ever since. Meanwhile, Orbitz lurks nearby—with a 17 percent share in 2004, compared to Travelocity's 20 percent—threatening to push the Sabre subsidiary to the number three spot. Insiders say Travelocity's decision to partner with hotels.com (rather than dealing directly with the hotels), sluggishness in developing combined vacation packages, and advertising agreement with AOL (which turned out to be much less profitable than expected) are all factors contributing to the travel agency's decline.

Turning the tide

Good news for Travelocity came in July 2004 when the company posted profits for the first time in two years. As of July 2005, Travelocity was still in the black—and growing revenue too. For the second quarter, the subsidiary posted sales of $172 million, a 37 percent increase from the second quarter of 2004. Although the company has significant work ahead if it wants to challenge Expedia for the number one spot, it is much better positioned than in previous years, thanks to a new philosophy, technology and business strategy. Travelocity's new technology system links directly to the reservation systems of individual hotels, eliminating the need for hotels to manually confirm reservations and giving customers added assurance that reservations are properly recorded. Other initiatives for the company include listing the full price for rental cars, including taxes and other fees which may add up to 25 percent of the standalone daily rate, and launching an $80 million ad campaign featuring the roaming gnome from the French movie *Amelie*. The gnome has become so popular that the company now offers all sorts of gnome merchandise, from coffee mugs to mouse pads.

Acquiring assets

Travelocity also got a boost from recent acquisitions, which include Travelocity Europe, SynXis Corp., Igougo.com and Lastminute.com. Adding to Travelocity's international reach, Sabre acquired the remaining 50 percent stake in Travelocity Europe in October 2004 and Lastminute.com, a U.K.-based provider of flights and vacation packages over the Internet in 13 countries, in May 2005. Stateside, Sabre bought SynXis Corp., a privately held provider of reservation management services for approximately 6,000 hotel properties, in December 2004, and Igougo.com, an online community where members post and retrieve firsthand travel experiences, in April 2005.

Tough times ahead

Insiders predict, however, that 2005 will be much more difficult for online travel companies. For one, the competition is heating up—and not just from the usual suspects. Major internet players, such as Yahoo! and AOL, are getting more involved in travel, and new players, such as G2 SwitchWorks and ITA Software, are emerging. Furthermore, Internet travel companies may have less access to inventory as travel suppliers (i.e. airlines) invest in their own web sites. Finally, analysts predict Travelocity and its competitors may see smaller markups from hoteliers and airlines.

On a more positive note, the online travel industry is definitely growing. By December 2004, the Travel Industry Association of America (TIA) says that 67 percent of travelers with Internet access plan and book trips online, due to a new generation of net savvy consumers. Furthermore, with a strong cash position of $474 million, parent company Sabre has the means to make acquisitions and bolster Travelocity's competitive positioning. Insiders point to Priceline.com as a good potential target for the travel conglomerate.

Visit Vault at **www.vault.com** for insider company profiles, expert advice, career message boards, expert resume reviews, the Vault Job Board and more.

VAULT CAREER LIBRARY   225

GETTING HIRED

Denim and T-shirts

The employment section of Travelocity's web site (see "About Travelocity" and then click on "Employment") boasts a "casual and comfortable workplace" where employees can wear jeans every day and shorts in the summer. The company also advertises an "above-average amount of time off" during which team members are encouraged to go out and see the world. Other perks range from health coverage, 401(k) savings plans and flexible work schedules to travel discounts and free vacations.

Sound like the place for you? Travelocity offers work opportunities in seven U.S. locations including the company's headquarters in Fort Worth, Texas. Prospective hires can search current job openings on Sabre's career site by entering in the keyword "Travelocity."

Tribe Networks Inc.

208 Utah Street
San Francisco, CA 94103
Phone: (415) 861-2286
Fax: (415) 861-5989
www.tribe.net

LOCATION

San Francisco, CA (HQ)

THE STATS

Employer Type: Private Company
CEO: Jan Gullett

KEY COMPETITORS

craigslist, inc.
Friendster
Meetup.com

EMPLOYMENT CONTACT

sanfrancisco.tribe.net

Visit Vault at **www.vault.com** for insider company profiles, expert advice,
career message boards, expert resume reviews, the Vault Job Board and more.

VAULT CAREER LIBRARY   227

THE SCOOP

Tribal connections

Tribe Networks is the driving force behind Tribe.net, which acts as a kind of Friendster-meets-craigslist for the Internet set. The site allows users to create profiles and to join networks, or "tribes," based on common interests. In addition, members can post listings for jobs, housing, events and even recommendations. Tribe serves 50 metropolitan markets, its largest being the San Francisco Bay Area, Los Angeles, Washington, D.C., and New York City.

The original online cocktail party

Mark Pincus, Paul Martino and Valerie Syme founded the firm in July 2003 with the goal of connecting local people for what Pincus described as "an online cocktail party where people are getting leads through their friends. So people are there to have fun and connect and meet new people." Pincus had previous experience with technology start-ups as the co-founder of Supportsoft, provider of enterprise support automation software, and founder of FreeLoader, maker of Internet software designed to load web pages faster.

Soon, the site had garnered the interest of Knight Ridder, The Washington Post Company and blue chip venture firm Mayfield, to the tune of $6.3 million in venture capital. Mayfield called the firm "a strong, early leader in trusted person-to-person online classifieds." Within three months of its founding, Tribe had amassed a network of over 48,000 registered users and 6,900 distinct tribes, earning revenue from job postings and classifieds. Tribe was even influential in the political arena, gathering "hundreds" of supporters for Matt Gonzalez, a candidate in the 2003 race for mayor in San Francisco.

Outrageous offerings

In March 2004, the firm entered into a partnership with CareerBuilder.com, allowing Tribe members to access CareerBuilder's job postings. Tribe's job postings are notorious, having garnered the firm some of its biggest publicity to date. Under the heading *OutRaGeouS* Tribe members can find postings for fire-breathing ministers, permanent snugglers, therapists well-versed in the art of improvisational gibberish and loud-mouths specializing in "bringing property values down."

Jan Gullett came aboard as CEO in 2005, replacing Pincus, who remained on Tribe's board. Gullett previously ran several consumer Internet companies after marketing stints at Sara Lee and Pepsico. Gullett's two main goals for the company are to "exponentially grow" Tribe's user base and to increase revenue.

GETTING HIRED

Homegrown heroes

Tribe uses its own job list, tribe.net, to seek out "good folks." The firm posts openings under the San Francisco Bay Area listings on tribe.net.

Visit Vault at **www.vault.com** for insider company profiles, expert advice,
career message boards, expert resume reviews, the Vault Job Board and more.

VAULT CAREER LIBRARY   229

VeriFone, Inc.

2099 Gateway Place, Suite 600
San Jose, CA 95110
Phone: (408) 232-7800
Fax: (408) 232-7811
www.verifone.com

LOCATIONS

San Jose, CA (HQ)
24 sales and marketing offices and
18 development centers in North
America, Latin America, the
Caribbean, Europe, Middle East,
Africa, Asia and the Pacific Rim.

THE STATS

Employer Type: Public Company
Stock Symbol: PAY
Stock Exchange: NYSE
Chairman & CEO: Douglas G. (Doug)
Bergeron
2004 Revenue ($mil.): $390.1

KEY COMPETITORS

Hypercom
Ingenico
NCR

EMPLOYMENT CONTACT

www.verifone.com/aboutus/careers/
index.cfm

THE SCOOP

POS-sibilities

VeriFone is a global leader in secure electronic payment technology, with over two decades of experience in point-of-sale (POS) transactions. The firm is one of the largest providers of electronic payment systems worldwide, with customers in more than 100 countries, including government agencies and companies in the hospitality, petroleum, retail and health care markets. The company also generates profit from installation, project management, training and other services.

A veritable e-commerce innovator

Founded in 1981 by William Melton, VeriFone initially focused on the development of electronic mail systems that enabled employees to correspond with their employers while on the road. By 1984 the company had diversified its product line to include automation transaction systems—specifically ZON, an electronic credit card and terminal for the verification of checks. Over the next six years the company's product development line shifted from hardware to software. By the time VeriFone went public in 1990, its focus was on software that connected computer terminals and printers. In 1991 the company released Gemstone transaction systems, a family of software products that electronically executed inventory and price checks as products were variously bought for sale, sold and returned. An electronic cash register constituted VeriFone's subsequent product. Released in 1992, the register could process credit and debit cards and verify checks. In 1999 the company split into two parts, with one focusing terminals and the other developing e-commerce software.

Going global at Verifone

The growing retail and consumer demand for the convenience offered by VeriFone's information processing systems led to the company's expansion to markets overseas. By 1994 VeriFone had offices in China, Hong Kong, Japan and South Africa. Business continued to grow steadily, with net income rising from $27.7 to $32.5 million from 1994 to 1995.

Visit Vault at www.vault.com for insider company profiles, expert advice, career message boards, expert resume reviews, the Vault Job Board and more.

VAULT CAREER LIBRARY   231

HP takes over, sort of

In 1997 the company was acquired by Hewlett-Packard for $1.29 billion, although it retains its status as an independent business entity. Several VeriFone executives left the company to join competing terminal vendors, coinciding with VeriFone's loss of market share in 1998 (although the company remained the leading terminal vendor by a wide margin). VeriFone was also an early purveyor of smart card technology (cards with tiny embedded chips, which analysts predict will replace the magnetic strip credit card in coming years) as well as new Internet payment methods. The introduction of the Omni 3200 terminal contributed to VeriFone's shipment of 8 million payment terminals in 1999. VeriFone introduced VeriTalk Lite that summer, an improvement on 1997's VeriFoneEnterprise, which downloads software to multiple terminals. In 2000 VeriFone expanded its Integrated Payment Solutions e-payment software with the addition of new applications that facilitate online transactions.

Independence granted

In May 2001, Gores Technology Group, a private firm, acquired VeriFone for an undisclosed amount. Gores' founder and chairman, Alec Gores, noted VeriFone had a "desperate need to be independent from a big company," and was poised for greatness with its smart card technology. Meanwhile, VeriFone was hard at work on system upgrades, launching the Omni 3600 wireless, multi-application payment terminal, the Omni 3210 with internal PINpad, and the Omni 3700 family of systems. In 2002, VeriFone teamed up with Shell Oil Products US as a strategic provider of point-of-sale (POS) systems. VeriFone also found success with the spread of quick service and "drive-thru" restaurants, which became a large growth area for payments.

Big year

The firm kept busy in 2004 with a number of deals both stateside and abroad. That May, VeriFone announced a joint project with McAfee to produce the industry's first virus protection solution for POS payment terminals, and also released Vx solutions, a next-generation payment solutions platform. On the corporate end, VeriFone signed with Burger King Corporation and Barnes & Noble to provide POS in all company-owned locations nationwide, and had a hand in the shift of the Food Stamps benefits program from a paper-based system to an electronic benefits transfer program. The firm also expanded its global presence by opening a regional headquarters in the Philippines, and even provided POS solutions to the Official Bank of the Athens 2004 Olympic Summer Games. By the end of the year, VeriFone had picked up the assets of GO Software from Return On Investment Corporation in a deal worth roughly $15 million, as part of a plan to expand into other integrated point-of-sale environments.

PAY day

Verifone, Inc. went public with an April 2005 IPO, listing on the NYSE under the ticker symbol "PAY." New products included the MX870 and Omni 7000LE, both secure payment systems for multi-lane retailers; VeriFone Connect, an all-inclusive, turnkey service enabling portable and countertop wireless POS payment; and IPCharge, a Web-based hosted payment processing solution. VeriFone also launched its Vx solutions across the Middle East in May 2005, and installed over 2,000 integrated POS systems at convenience stores owned by Valero Energy Corp. nationwide in August 2005. The same month, the firm also announced a partnership with Cold Stone Creamery to equip franchises with Omni 3750 payment solutions for a nationwide electronic gift card program.

In the third quarter reported that August, VeriFone recorded a net income of $6.5, compared with a loss of $2.9 million the year prior, while revenue increased 21 percent from $104 million to $125.7 million.

GETTING HIRED

Verifine opportunities

The company posts available job opportunities on its web site at www.verifone.com. Job listings are configured so that prospective job seekers can search openings by category or location, and send VeriFone their resume electronically.

OUR SURVEY SAYS

The caring company

The most common adjective VeriFone employees use to describe their company is caring. The most important part of the work atmosphere, says one insider, is that VeriFone cares for its employees. "We are better paid than most other companies in the industry, and VFI provides us with the best of office, sports and games facilities. The dress code is informal, the workers friendly, and with respect to [the company's

Visit Vault at **www.vault.com** for insider company profiles, expert advice, career message boards, expert resume reviews, the Vault Job Board and more.

VAULT CAREER LIBRARY   **233**

treatment] of minorities and women everyone is treated as a wonderful human being!" VeriFone has written a book on its philosophy toward employees and customers, and, as one worker comments, it "follows it to the core." Working hours tend to be flexible because, as one worker explains, "VeriFone started in Hawaii and a lot of [its relaxed] attitudes remain to date."

"I enjoy every moment working here"

"The company's most attractive feature is its caring, open culture," which, combined with "good to excellent salaries," prompts one insider to claim that "I enjoy every moment working here," an expansive declaration indeed. So if you're interested in computer science and its applications to the electronic processing of information, VeriFone might well be the place for you.

WebMD, Inc.

111 Eighth Avenue, 7th Floor
New York, NY 10011
Phone: (212) 624-3700
Fax: (212) 624-3800
www.webmd.com

LOCATION
New York, NY (HQ)

DEPARTMENTS
Offline Print
Private Health Portals
Public Health Portals

THE STATS

Employer Type: Subsidiary of
Emdeon
Stock Symbol: WBMD
Stock Exchange: NASDAQ
President and CEO: Wayne T.
Gattinella
2004 Employees: Approx. 550
2004 Revenue ($mil.): $134.1

KEY COMPETITORS

iVillage
Mayo Foundation
Medsite

EMPLOYMENT CONTACT

www.webmdcareers.net

THE SCOOP

Name game

WebMD, Inc. is the public and private portal division of Emdeon Corporation (previously WebMD Corporation). Best known for its consumer health information web site, WebMD provides health information services to consumers, physicians and health care professionals, employers and health plans through its public and private portals. The subsidiary also publishes supplementary offline content.

The company formerly known as WebMD Corporation changed its name to Emdeon Corporation on August 5, 2005 to avoid confusion with its subsidiary WebMD Health Corp. (now WebMD, Inc.), which began trading on the Nasdaq as a separately traded company on September 29, 2005, under the symbol WBMD.

WebMD and beyond

Through the company's primary web site, WebMD.com, visitors can find a doctor, check symptoms, learn about common illnesses and diseases, get answers to questions from real physicians, or chat with others about medical conditions. WedMD also offers subscription services—WebMD Weight Loss Clinic, WebMD Health Manager and WebMD Fertility Center—and a new magazine, *WebMD*, launched in April 2005. Aimed at consumers, the magazine is distributed bimonthly in the waiting rooms of approximately 85 percent of physicians' offices across the country.

While WebMD.com targets consumers, Medscape.com from WebMD caters to physicians and health care professionals. Through the site, users can access more than 100 medical journals, specialty-specific daily medical news, online coverage of medical conferences and online continuing medical education (CME).

Awarded

Over the years, WebMD has racked up quite a following (more than 24 million consumers visit the site each month) and more than a few awards. In 2004, the site won a Silver Medal in the category of Patient Education Information for its Symptom Checker and a Bronze Medal in the category of Health Promotion/Disease Prevention for its Talking to Your Teen from the World Wide Health Awards. The e-Healthcare Leadership Awards presented the site with a Gold Medal for "Best Health Content" and a Silver Medal for "Best Overall Internet Site" and *PC Magazine* named WebMD

Visit Vault at **www.vault.com** for insider company profiles, expert advice, career message boards, expert resume reviews, the Vault Job Board and more.

VAULT CAREER LIBRARY   **237**

one of the top 10 search, reference and portal sites of the year. The site also earned first place in the category of Non-Deadline Reporting from the Society of Professional Journalists in 2003 and 2004 for its special reports on *What's Happening to Our Kids* and *Wired Health: At Your Fingertips*.

GETTING HIRED

Find a match

Individuals interested in working for WebMD should visit www.webmdcareers.net, the general careers site for Emdeon. Here, candidates can choose a quick search — by keyword, professional area or date posted — or a more advanced search, which allows applicants to select amount of travel (none, constant, minimal or moderate) and employment status (full time or part time). Postings include a detailed description of job responsibilities and list of requirements. Candidates who don't find an opening matching their skill level or interests are encouraged to create an online profile and attach a resume for future opportunities.

Wind River Inc.

500 Wind River Way
Alameda, CA 94501-1171
Phone: (510) 748-4100
Fax: (510) 749-2010
www.windriver.com

LOCATION

Alameda, CA (HQ)

DEPARTMENTS

Corporate Marketing
Engineering
Finance
Product Marketing
Professional Service Cost
Sales
Software Development
Supply Chain

THE STATS

Employer Type: Public Company
Stock Symbol: WIND
Stock Exchange: NASDAQ
Chairman & CEO: Kenneth (Ken) R. Klein
2005 Employees: 1,112
2005 Revenue ($mil.): $235.4

KEY COMPETITORS

Green Hills Software
Microsoft
QNX Software

EMPLOYMENT CONTACT

careers-windriver.com/windriver/job
  board/default.asp

THE SCOOP

Like the wind

Wind River makes operating systems and tools used in device software such as PDAs, set top boxes, automotive controls, pacemakers and robotics. Wind River is the global leader in device software optimization (DSO). The company's products serve several key markets including automotive, consumer, defense, industrial and network infrastructure. More than 300 million of the world's most sophisticated devices run on Wind River device software. Several of its clients include heavy hitters across those sectors, such as Cisco, Ericsson, Lockheed-Martin, Intel and Nortel.

Blowing into new markets

Jerry Fiddler, known in some circles as the "father of embedded software," founded Wind River in 1981, and formally incorporated the company two years later. In 1987, Wind River launched its VxWorks operating system, which helps customers standardize designs and cut down research and development costs. The company went public in 1994; the following year marked the debut of Tornado, a development platform that helps customers test their own products. In 1998, the company acquired Zinc Software, a graphics application company. It also gained Internet connectivity technology from NCI (known now as Liberate, in which Wind River invested in 1999).

Taking a roller coaster ride

In 2000, Wind River bought Integrated Systems Inc. and related subsidiaries for $1 billion. Today the company operates in 20 countries around the globe. Taking a roller coaster ride like other tech companies, Wind River enjoyed heady profits and stock gains during the Internet boom that dominated the late 1990s and into the new millennium. In the year that ended in January 2001, the company posted $438 million in revenue, up from $171 million the prior year. But as companies curtailed their tech-related spending and the tech bubble burst, Wind River found itself hard hit. Its stock slumped and the company cut some staff in 2001 in an effort to control costs. Still, the tech market proved to be a rocky one to navigate, and for the year that ended in January 2002, Wind River posted a loss of $375 million. In May 2002, the company said it would reduce operating expenses by $4 million to $6 million a quarter, in part by eliminating 320 jobs. In August 2002, Wind River met lowered expectations on Wall Street, reporting a net loss for its second quarter of just under $37 million, down from a year earlier loss of $281.6 million. Revenue dropped 21 percent year over year to $63.6 million.

Sent down the river

In November 2002, Wind River announced a plan to bundle its technology and services into four platforms to be sold through subscriptions, rather than per project. The decision to bundle products came out of the the desire to offer a product to clients that could help them operate more efficiently. Despite such forward-thinking, Wind River still continued to miss financial marks, as revenue slipped 27 percent in the quarter ended April 2003. Two months later, then-president and CEO Tom St. Dennis was asked to step down.

Klein meets his match

Ken Klein was named president, CEO and chairman that November. Klein was previously the chief operating officer of Mercury Interactive Corp., a business technology optimization company. He had initially been brought on to the Wind River board over the summer of 2003 to help find a replacement for St. Dennis—but ended up "falling in love" with the company and its clients, and soon positioned himself in the driver's seat, determined to guide Wind River to success despite the complicated market.

One of Klein's first big moves was a partnership with leading Linux distributor Red Hat Inc., announced in February 2004, to jointly develop Red Hat Embedded Linux. In addition, Red Hat's Linux would serve as the foundation for Wind River Linux-based platforms and would be integrated with Wind River's tools and services. Klein noted the deal had the potential to become "the most important third-party relationship in Wind River's history," and stock jumped 15 percent on the news.

Wind sails to Linux

Though best known for its flagship VxWorks products and solutions, the company's entrance into the Linux space has been very successful. When Klein assumed his current position, Wind River was without a Linux strategy. Klein quickly acted upon the market opportunity offered by Linux. As the company changed its tune on Linux under Klein's orchestration, customers have responded. Linux growth for Wind River is 600 percent year-over-year and its market share has increased by 34 percent.

Visit Vault at **www.vault.com** for insider company profiles, expert advice, career message boards, expert resume reviews, the Vault Job Board and more.

VAULT CAREER LIBRARY   241

In October 2005, Wind River announced its Linux device software platform for consumer devices, rounding out the industry's best commercial-grade quality Linux product line. Wind River's Linux platform now scales to support a full range of device requirements from handhelds to network equipment, with over 50 technology partnerships.

Working out a compromise

At the start of 2005, Green Hills Software Inc. filed a lawsuit against Wind River, after the latter attempted to quit a 99-year cooperative agreement between the two companies before the time limit was up. The other company also accused Wind River of monopolizing a segment of the market by blocking Green Hills' attempts to get updates to Wind River's VxWorks operating system. The two later settled in June 2005, after Wind River agreed to provide Green Hills with its VxWorks system in object code form.

Model student

For the fiscal year 2005, Wind River posted a 16 percent year-over-year increase in revenue, climbing to $251.7 million. Stock reached a new 52-week high on the news. The subscription-based services plan first developed in 2002 helped the firm increase cash flow and deferred revenue to the tune of $76.7 million, a 96 percent increase over the year prior. Klein said of the smashing results, "We received our report card, and it's an A."

Overseas, Wind River also deepened its partnership with Wipro Ltd., India's third-largest software company, as part of an effort to increase the use of its operating system (which runs a tight second to Microsoft's system for so-called embedded device software) on a global scale. As part of the deal, Wind River agreed to pass off potential services customers to Wipro, which, in turn agreed to continue using Wind River's platform, and also to recommend the platform to its own customers.

GETTING HIRED

Putting some Wind in your sail

Visit the career section of the company's web site at careers-windriver.com/ windriver/jobboard/default.asp to view job opportunities online and submit applications. Wind River also accepts resumes (along with the position desired, salary requirements and relocation information) via e-mail at resumes@careers-windriver.com or by regular old postal service:

Wind River Systems
Attn: Staffing Department
500 Wind River Way
Alameda, CA 94501

Visit Vault at **www.vault.com** for insider company profiles, expert advice,
career message boards, expert resume reviews, the Vault Job Board and more.

VΛULT CAREER LIBRARY   **243**

XO Communications, Inc.

11111 Sunset Hills Road
Reston, VA 20190-5339
Phone: (703) 547-2000
Fax: (703) 547-2881
www.xo.com

LOCATION

Reston, VA (HQ)

THE STATS

Employer Type: Public Company
Stock Symbol: XOCM
Stock Exchange: OTC
Chairman: Carl C. Icahn
CEO: Carl J. Grivner
2004 Employees: 5,000
2004 Revenue ($mil.): $1,300.4

KEY COMPETITORS

AT&T
Qwest
Verizon

EMPLOYMENT CONTACT

www.xo.com/about/careers

THE SCOOP

Networking success

Working with small and mid-sized businesses, XO Communications, a competitive local-exchange carrier (CLEC), made an early name for itself by investing in the development of metropolitan fiber-optic ring networks connected by a Tier 1 fiber backbone network stretching across the U.S. But after its cash supply ran dry, the company was forced to undergo Chapter 11 bankruptcy protection in June 2002, emerging in 2003 after financier Carl Icahn took a controlling share.

Today, XO offers a number of access options for small and growing businesses, including fiber direct to buildings, DSL (digital subscriber line), and fixed-wireless technologies. XO also provides local and long-distance phone services and—thanks to its acquisition of Concentric Network—offers Internet services. The company bills itself as "one of the only national, local end-to-end broadband communications companies in the U.S.," with a fiber and wireless broadband communications network serving 63 metro markets across the nation. XO is also one of North America's biggest holders of fixed broadband wireless spectrum, with licenses covering 95 percent of the population of the 30 largest U.S. cities.

Too much too soon?

Formed in September 2000 through the merger of broadband provider Nextlink Communications and Concentric Networks, XO Communications emerged as a leader in the telecommunications sector. In December 2001, Telfonos de Mexico S.A. de C.V., Mexico's largest telecommunications company, and Forstmann Little, an investment firm, infused the firm with a total of $800 million in exchange for equity, as XO struggled to develop its broadband networks while boosting its bottom line. However, XO's growing debt—$8.5 billion at its height—forced the firm to file for bankruptcy in June 2002. Chairman and CEO Daniel Akerson left soon after that December to pursue other business interests.

Icahn-do attitude

By the start of 2003, XO had emerged from bankruptcy reorganization with the help of financier Carl Icahn, who became both chairman and majority owner, holding 85 percent of XO's senior debt and more than $1.3 billion of its senior notes. Debt shrunk to a mere $500 million, and Icahn put in place a plan to grow business through

Visit Vault at **www.vault.com** for insider company profiles, expert advice, career message boards, expert resume reviews, the Vault Job Board and more.

V∧ULT CAREER LIBRARY   **245**

acquisition. One of its first post-Chapter 11 contracts was with G.A. Sullivan, developer of software for insurance, banking and securities firms, to provide voice and data communications services for an undisclosed amount. A $1.5 million deal with Hitachi Metals America to serve as Hitachi's primary data network provider soon followed. Carl Grivner, a former executive at Global Crossing, signed on as CEO in April 2003, and took on the additional jobs of president and chief operating officer the following month from the departing Nate Davis.

New business

In February 2004, the firm applied to list its common shares on the Nasdaq Market; shares were being traded on the over-the-counter market since the firm's emergence from bankruptcy. CEO Grivner said a Nasdaq listing would help the company expand through the use of cash and stock. The same month, XO made good on its promise to grow through acquisition, picking up Dallas-based Allegiance Telecom for $631 million, outbidding rival Qwest Communications. The deal was a big one for XO, adding over 100,000 customers and significant presence in a number of new markets, and also boosting annual revenue past $1.6 billion. Despite the wheeling and dealing, XO reported lower revenue and wider first-quarter losses in May 2004 compared with year-ago results.

Scoring fans

A year later, XO bounced back with its nationwide Voice over Internet Protocol bundle for businesses, called XOptions Flex, which combined unlimited local and long-distance calling, dedicated Internet access, and web hosting services for a flat monthly fee. XO also signed deals with the Seattle Mariners and Sacramento Kings in 2004 and 2005, respectively, to become the teams' "official telecommunications provider," offering local voice, long-distance voice, and data services to the teams' front offices, stores and training complexes. More recently, XO rolled out its Wholesale Local Voice services platform in September 2005 to support competitive CLECs in competition with regional Bell operating companies. The company's books reflect the new business: second-quarter revenue in the fiscal year 2004 increased 30 percent to $362.2 million, while the firm generated a positive net cash flow of $13.5 million.

GETTING HIRED

Application 411

XO posts job openings on its career web site, www.xo.com/about/careers. Applicants can search for positions by keyword, location and type.

Visit Vault at **www.vault.com** for insider company profiles, expert advice,
career message boards, expert resume reviews, the Vault Job Board and more.

VAULT CAREER LIBRARY   247

Yahoo! Inc.

701 1st Avenue
Sunnyvale, CA 94089
Phone: (408) 349-3300
Fax: (408) 349-3301
www.yahoo.com

LOCATION

Sunnyvale, CA (HQ)
Offices in Europe, Asia, Latin
America, Australia and Canada.

THE STATS

Employer Type: Public Company
Stock Symbol: YHOO
Stock Exchange: NASDAQ
Chairman & CEO: Terry S. Semel
2004 Employees: 9,600
2004 Revenue ($mil.): $3,574.5

KEY COMPETITORS

America Online
Google
MSN

EMPLOYMENT CONTACT

careers.yahoo.com

THE SCOOP

The fairy tale

Founded in 1994 by David Filo and Jerry Yang, two Stanford graduate students looking for a way to index their favorite web sites, Yahoo! met with almost instant success as an Internet search engine, attracting tens of thousands of web users searching for their favorite pages. Indeed, about four months after starting the site, Yahoo! was getting 100,000 hits a day, and later that year celebrated its first million-hit day. The company quickly moved on to receive its first round of funding in April 1995, and launched its IPO in April 1996. In keeping with the intense dot-com zeitgeist, the newly public company had just 49 employees. As of October 2005, the company had grown to 9,600 employees. For the 2004 fiscal year, Yahoo! brought in revenue of $3.5 billion.

Obviously, Yahoo! still has legions of fans. So why have users stuck with the site when so many other search engines have dropped off the radar? Well, they're not logging on just for the search engine. Today, users can use Yahoo! to access the latest news, financial information and streaming media. The site also offers registered users personalized web pages, e-mail, chat rooms and message boards. With 15 languages in 25 global regions, and with over 411 million unique visitors, Yahoo! is the No.-1 Internet brand globally.

Growing by leaps and bounds

By January 1999, Yahoo! had grown large enough to purchase GeoCities for $3.6 billion, and in April, bought Broadcast.com for $5.7 billion. The purchase of GeoCities allowed Yahoo! to begin offering paying customers the capability to create their own web sites, while the Broadcast acquisition gave Yahoo! a leading edge in the multimedia sector and allowed the company to integrate Broadcast's streaming media into its other web offerings. Throughout the rest of 1999 and 2000, the company was busy rolling out new features, including an instant messenger, and health, entertainment, finance, employment, auctions, radio, shopping and games channels. Then in early 2002, the company made a major move, when it acquired career site Hotjobs.com for $436 million. The deal gave Yahoo! a huge leg up in the highly lucrative online job search field. In January 2003 Yahoo! introduced its first music subscription service, LAUNCHcast Plus.

Visit Vault at **www.vault.com** for insider company profiles, expert advice, career message boards, expert resume reviews, the Vault Job Board and more.

VAULT CAREER LIBRARY   249

Innovations

In 2000, Yahoo! became the first major Internet company to unveil a direct investment plan, allowing people to buy Yahoo! shares without a broker. Later that year, the company purchased Online Anywhere, a software company that enables web pages to be sent to cell phones and personal digital assistants. Yahoo! also struck a marketing and distribution deal with Sprint Corporation, through which it delivers e-mail, stock quotes, news and other information to Sprint PCS users. These agreements, along with one announced in 2000 with AT&T, formed the basic elements of the company's Yahoo!Mobile offering, which has allowed it to extend its reach beyond the desktop.

A rough patch

Things haven't always been so rosy, however. Although Yahoo! was never in any danger of going bust like a lot of other dot-coms, it wasn't immune to the effects of the economic downturn. In April 2001, the company announced that its quarterly earnings were going to fall short—or at best just break even—with previous expectations. As part of a broad reorganization, the company announced that it was going to reduce the number of its 3,510 employees by approximately 12 percent, and in April cut 400 people from the company's payroll. Tim Koogle also announced his resignation after six years as CEO.

Enter an unlikely hero: Terry Semel, a former executive at the Warner Bros. movie studio. Industry insiders viewed Semel as a "strange" choice for CEO, given his experience in the entertainment industry, not the Internet. At a press conference following his hiring in April 2001, Semel called himself "a builder" and noted he was "totally excited about building Yahoo! as a brand and building it into a bigger and better company." Yahoo! no doubt hoped Semel would channel some of his prior business building at Warner Bros. where, along with partner Bob Daly, he grew the business from $750 million in revenue to $11 billion over a 19-year period.

Turning the corner

By the third quarter of 2001, the company was reporting losses of $24 million. By the end of the year, the company saw revenue of just $717 million, down from $1.1 billion in 2000. But the company really turned the corner in 2002 thanks to the reorganization and the eventual payoff of the company's many acquisitions in 2000 and 2001 (including HotJobs.com). Earnings for the year were $206 million compared with a loss of $18.6 million in 2001, and income for the year was $106 million, compared to a loss of $92 million in 2001.

The Internet is dead, long live the Internet!

While plenty of fly-by-night Internet operations bit the dust after the big 2000-2001 market shakeout, Yahoo! stuck to its guns and according to Nielsen/NetRatings, was the most visited global Internet destination in 2002. In the same year, the company's global audience grew to approximately 213 million users, while Yahoo!'s active registered users (those who log in with a username and password) grew twice as fast to approximately 101 million—representing a 37 percent year-over-year increase. Although the company still makes most of its money through advertising, it has done a great job in diversifying revenue streams. In January 2002, Yahoo! had 375,000 paying relationships, which means those who had signed up to pay for extra e-mail space, paid personals (Yahoo! is now the largest personals site on the Internet), Fantasy Sports and Games on Demand. By the end of the year, however, the company had bumped the number of paying relationships up to 2.2 million people

Still going strong

In 2003, Yahoo! was still plugging along, maintaining profitability. In the second quarter 2003, the company saw revenue of $321 million, a 42 percent increase over the $225 million reported for the same period in 2002. Likewise, operating income for the second quarter was $62.8 million, compared to $7.5 million for the same period of 2002. For the first half of 2003, revenue totaled $604 million, a 44 percent increase over the $418 million reported for the same period in 2002. Operating income for the first half of the year stood at $117 million, compared to $3.3 million for same period of 2002.

Searching for themselves

In November 2003, Yahoo! altered its home page to highlight specialized search features, in a likely bid to drive traffic to the new tools and recapture ground from rival search engine Google. Although Yahoo! had been licensing Google's algorithmic search technology for its web search function, the company showed its eagerness to strike out on its own (and perhaps recapture the mantle of most popular search engine on the Internet) when it acquired search technology company Inktomi for $235 million in March.

In July 2003, Yahoo! acquired web search products AltaVista and Alltheweb.com through its $1.7 billion acquisition of Overture Services, an Internet "commercial search service" that pioneered the somewhat controversial practice of commercial search by aligning the interests of its 88,000 active, paying advertisers and its distribution partners, including Yahoo!, MSN and CNN. What it boils down to is that the platform allows marketers to pay for inclusion on an Internet search index, instead of page hits being the determining factor in a search. The impetus is largely fueled by the shifting economics of searching and its lucrative advertising component, pay-per-click sponsored listings. As a result of such listings, the search market is expected to surge in value and has drawn the attention of numerous competitors, including software behemoth Microsoft. The Overture purchase gave Yahoo! a solid foundation in the online advertising space.

Reaping the rewards

Yahoo! has evolved from a company that relied on a single revenue source dominated by dot-com advertisers, to a business with more diverse and sustainable sources of revenue. Yahoo! has used its subscription-based premium services to draw revenue directly from millions of users. Yahoo! also makes money from hundreds of blue-chip advertisers and thousands of small- and medium-sized businesses. This depth of revenue streams helped the company record unprecedented revenue in 2003. Sales for 2003 totaled $1.6 billion, an increase of more than 70 percent over 2002. Yahoo! also grew its balance sheet throughout the year to $2.5 billion, despite spending a large amount of money the Inktomi and Overture acquisitions.

Growing its fee-based services, Yahoo! ended 2003 approaching five million paying users, a 123 percent increase from approximately 2.2 million at the end of 2002. This is the fastest growing subset of users on the Yahoo! network. Access bundled with Yahoo! content, through relationships with SBC and British Telecommunications (BT), is the largest contributor. In September 2003, the company launched broadband operations in the U.K. through its partnership with BT and extended its agreement with SBC in November 2004. Yahoo! also has an alliance with Canadian cable provider Rogers Cable.

Yahoo! around the world

Thanks to the region-specific offshoots of Yahoo!, the company is the biggest portal in Europe, providing unique sites for several countries in a variety of languages and allowing users to limit web searches to sites based in that country.

Suit settled and the video stream runs dry

In August 2004, Yahoo! settled a two-year long dispute with fellow online giant (and rival) Google. In exchange for 2.7 million shares, Yahoo dropped the lawsuit, which claimed that Google infringed on the company's patents for the technology that matches advertising with search engine results. As part of the settlement, Yahoo! agreed to license said technology to Google for continued use. Also in 2004, Yahoo! put an end to its Yahoo! Platinum streaming video services, as interest had become miniscule. Instead, the company introduced Yahoo! Plus, a package containing e-mail service (including 10 different accounts) and video news streams. The product was designed to compete with similar services offered by AOL and Microsoft.

Full-speed ahead

Recording its sixth consecutive quarter of record sales, Yahoo! posted $907 million in revenue for the third quarter of 2004, up more than 150 percent compared to 2003. Revenue from the United States in the third quarter of 2004 grew to $655 million, an increase of $355 million, or 118 percent, compared to the same period in 2003. Internationally, revenue totaled $252 million for the third quarter of 2004, up 341 percent compared to the corresponding quarter in 2003.

Continuing its online onslaught throughout 2004, the company launched a new and improved version of its instant messenger service and remained acquisitive. Yahoo! has bought pan-European shopping comparison provider Kelkoo for $575 million and music software leader Musicmatch for $160 million. Additionally, the company entered the burgeoning Chinese market when it launched Yisou, and Internet search portal.

Bringing in the heavy hitters

Yahoo! made a couple of major personnel moves in November 2004 when the company hired Lloyd Braun, a former ABC executive, oversee its media and entertainment division and former *Wall Street Journal* publisher Neil Budde to run its news operations.

Birthday celebration

For the firm's tenth birthday in March 2005, co-founder Yang announced a number of new Yahoo! products in development, including Y!Q, which lets users do a contextual search on any block of text on any web page; a local search service that includes interactive maps and real-time traffic updates; and a desktop search tool,

Visit Vault at **www.vault.com** for insider company profiles, expert advice, career message boards, expert resume reviews, the Vault Job Board and more.

VAULT CAREER LIBRARY 253

currently in beta testing. Yang also sees opportunity to capitalize on the blogging craze, and to provide more content for broadband wireless users. Meanwhile, CEO Semel praised the firm for its "terrific start" to 2005, as it topped Wall Street estimates and raised guidance, due to increased profit from advertising, Yahoo!'s largest revenue generator.

Building a media empire

Yahoo! has long claimed it is a "media empire in the making," though critics have likened the firm more to a utilities company than anything else. Yahoo! looked to silence the naysayers during the summer of 2005, as Semel signed off on a slew of deals designed to expand its offerings beyond simple search and e-mail. In June 2005, Yahoo! entered into a joint venture with Sprint Corp. to launch a pay e-mail service for mobile phone customers, and acquired Dialpad Communications, an Internet telephony company, to allow calling between computers and standard telephones.

Then, that August, ABC News and CNN announced plans to provide video news feeds to Yahoo!'s news site; while Yahoo! signed a deal with Viacom to provide search-marketing and web-search services to Viacom's online properties, including CBS News and MTV.com, and paired up with Verizon Communications to offer cheaper high-speed Internet service to compete against cable operators and dial-up service providers. The company also released a new web service to allow users to search the Internet for music and other audio, dubbed Yahoo! Audio Search.

Perhaps the firm's biggest purchase of all, though, was its $1 billion deal with Alibaba.com Corp., a Chinese e-commerce company, that made Yahoo! the company's largest single shareholder, with a 40 percent stake. Under terms of the deal, Alibaba will run Yahoo!'s search sites and brand in China, which is expected to surpass the U.S. in online population within the next few years.

Beating Google

Google continues to be the main thorn in Yahoo!'s side as the latter makes strides to maintain its position as a dominant search engine. In August 2005, Yahoo! announced it would expand the number of sites on which it places ads through a new service called Yahoo Publisher Network, as part of a plan to battle Google's stranglehold on the text-ads-linked-to-search-terms market. By the end of the month, Yahoo! had also added new search features to its e-mail service to help users manage messages, digital photos, files and other attachments, including a keyword search.

GETTING HIRED

An abundance of opportunities

Today, with more than 9,600 employees all over the world, Yahoo! has job opportunities galore. The company maintains an employment site at careers.yahoo.com, where potential employees can search through a list of available positions throughout the company by location, job title, job function and keyword search. Candidates can also electronically submit a profile or a resume/CV without applying to a specific job by creating an account on the career site. For those who don't see a specific job that catches their eye, Yahoo! accepts resumes for the future via e-mail at careers@yahoo-inc.com.

The company offers internships to college students. Be prepared to perform real work, not the "busy work" that some companies are known for foisting off on their interns. As the company's web site boasts, "At Yahoo! we don't believe in placing our interns in front of a photocopy machine or in an office filing all day. Our interns make an impact on the frontlines of our business." Additionally, Yahoo! recruits recent grads for a variety of functions, including sales, marketing, customer care and business development. Check the career site for more information on both internships and full-time positions for new grads.

OUR SURVEY SAYS

Kooky job titles and a loose atmosphere

Yahoo! boasts an "informal atmosphere" and a staff with "substantial industry expertise." A young company, Yahoo! offers employees a "dynamic" environment and the promise of "explosive growth" and potential riches through stock options. One contact praises the "approachable" staff and says that "Filo and Yang are down-to-earth guys. Everyone likes everyone a lot." Another insider points out that "even the biggies just have plain desks like everyone else." One employee says that she brings her pet parakeet to work "and that nobody cares. Except me and the bird." However, employees point out that Yahoo! is "navigating uncharted territory." Employees are confident that Yahoo!'s "fame among Internet users worldwide" will bring "permanent prestige" to their resumes. Insiders say they love the "kooky job titles and loose atmosphere."

Visit Vault at **www.vault.com** for insider company profiles, expert advice, career message boards, expert resume reviews, the Vault Job Board and more.

V∧ULT CAREER LIBRARY   255

About the Editor

Laurie Pasiuk graduated from Fordham University with a degree in English literature. She started and edited the fiction section for Elsevier Science's HMS *Beagle* before joining Vault as a staff editor.

GO FOR THE GOLD!

GET VAULT GOLD MEMBERSHIP AND GET ACCESS TO ALL OF VAULT'S AWARD-WINNING CAREER INFORMATION

◆ **Employee surveys for 4,000+ top employers,** with insider info on
  - Firm culture
  - Salaries and compensation
  - Hiring process and interviews
  - Business outlook

◆ Access to **1,000+ extended insider employer snapshots**

◆ **Student and alumni surveys** for 100s of top MBA programs, law schools and graduate school programs and 1000s of undergraduate programs

◆ Access to **Vault's Salary Central**, with salary information for law, finance and consulting firms

◆ Access to **complete Vault message board archives**

◆ **15% off** all Vault purchases, including Vault Guides, Employer Profiles and Vault Career Services (named the Wall Street Journal's "Top Choice" for resume makeovers)

For more information go to
www.vault.com

VAULT
> the most trusted name in career informatio